London

Dan Colwell

CITYSCAPE

JPMGUIDES

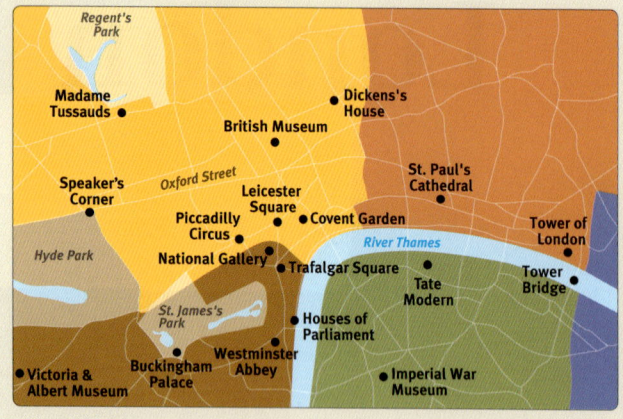

Most of London's famous sights are concentrated within the historic centre. The City is a mere square mile in size, and its ancient streets packed with renowned landmarks can be easily explored on foot. While there's nothing like poking around London's back streets in your own time, for an initial—and relaxed—way to get the lie of the land, take a tour on one of the double-decker sightseeing buses snaking their way through the city.

Contents

Features
Before the Flames:
London's Early
Architecture 24
Children's London 36
Shopper's London 48
Market Economies 56
What's in a Name? 66
Mine's a Pint! 74
London on the
Big Screen 99

Maps
The City 113
Central London 114
Docklands 116
Southwest London 118

Fold-out maps
London
Underground

Our favourite sights are marked with a star ★ in the table at the beginning of each section.

cityLights 5
cityPast 9
citySights 15
■ The City 16
■ West End 26
■ Westminster 38
■ South Bank 58
■ East End and Docklands .. 68
■ Excursions 76
cityBites 87
cityNights 95
cityFacts 103
Index 119

cityLights

You may well fall in love with London—but not necessarily at first sight. It can seem almost too big, too busy to start with. But one of the world's most liveable, most lovable great cities soon grows on you. The attractions add up: the elegance of a Georgian house, the details of a Victorian pub, a brave show of colour in a window box of geraniums, a gleaming brass doorknocker. All at once an accumulation of discreet charms will come into focus, and you'll discover that just being in this immensely civilized city makes you feel good.

London's diversity strikes visitors at once. The great governmental, financial and cultural centre is not really a city at all, but a cluster of villages—Chiswick, Hampstead, Chelsea, and so on, surrounding the City, the original walled town. One look at the streets and you read at a glance the colourful story of a land of immigration.

Today, against stiff competition, London hangs onto its title of most important financial centre of Europe, and businesspeople from all corners of the globe swarm to it as bees to honey. So do young people, drawn by the vibrant atmosphere of a city at the cutting edge of popular culture. The capital of the United Kingdom leads the way with the latest trends in rock and pop music, nightclubbing and street fashions.

For other visitors, the classical arts are the city's greatest draw: opera, ballet, orchestral and chamber music, theatre and, of course, several world-class museums.

Traditional yet modern

It may be young at heart, yet London still clings nostalgically to the old and traditional. However, there's hardly a bowler hat or furled umbrella to be seen, nowadays.

London has been changing physically, too; a building boom has altered its profile, inserting lofty, proud towers of steel and glass between the stone and red-brick Georgian and Victorian houses. Consider the breathtaking Lloyds Building, Norman Foster's gleaming new City Hall on the Southbank, or the dazzling development of the Docklands area. Earlier attempts at contemporary architecture, now much derided, are being replaced or renovated, and the city blazed a trail into the new millennium, with special attractions inaugurated in the year 2000 such as the rotating British Airways London Eye on the banks of the Thames, now one of the city's most popular "monuments". The more controversial Millennium Dome at Greenwich, renamed O$_2$, is now used as an indoor sports arena.

Green peace

A quick glance at the map shows that nearly as much land in London seems to be given over to parks as to buildings. Most of them were acquired on behalf of the London public many years ago, and are a jealously guarded privilege. You can take time off from sightseeing to feed the ducks or the pigeons and sparrows or to have a picnic in green and pleasant surroundings. All this right in the heart of the city.

Don't feel shy. It will be easy to strike up a conversation with the Londoner sitting beside you in the bus or sharing your park bench, who may be a true Cockney, born within sound of Bow Bells, an office worker enjoying a lunch break, a banker of old family lineage or an Indian doctor. Although they are as diverse in character as the city of villages they live in, Londoners share a hospitable manner, an easy-going nature and a developed sense of humour. They will sometimes go to great lengths to be of assistance. Seize the chance to get to know them better; your encounters with the people will almost certainly count among your most enduring memories of this unique and vibrant city.

SAVED BY THE BELL

The iconic clock tower of the Houses of Parliament is often referred to as Big Ben, though it's actually St Stephen's Tower. In fact, the real Big Ben is the massive 13-ton bell that sits behind the clock face. It's thought that the name refers to Sir Benjamin Hall, the large-framed Commissioner of Works at the time of the bell's inauguration in 1857. An equally compelling theory is that it's in honour of Benjamin Caunt, a boxer who weighed in at 115 kilos and won an epic 60-round fight the same year.

cityPast

Roman London

Julius Caesar had made reconnaissance raids on Britain in around 55–54 BC, but a century later the Romans were seriously thinking about putting down roots. In AD 43 Emperor Claudius launched a full-scale invasion and, with the intention of striking at the powerful Catuvellauni tribe's stronghold at Colchester, sought out the best crossing point over the Thames. He chose a site the local Celtic inhabitants called Llyn-Din, and latinized it to Londinium. The wooden bridge put up here by the Romans was not far from modern-day London Bridge.

With major roads soon radiating from the military garrison and ships calling regularly, it was inevitable that merchants would soon stream in. Londinium rapidly became one of the most prosperous towns in the Empire and was eventually elected administrative capital of Roman Britain in place of Colchester.

Around AD 200, the Romans built a defensive wall around the town, sectioning off a semicircular area of about a square mile, corresponding to the City financial district today.

During the 5th century, the Romans abandoned Londinium, now much in decline, and the city entered a dark, confused period, leaving it vulnerable to invasion.

Barbarians come to stay

The native Celts at first welcomed the new invaders—Angles, Saxons and Jutes—but were then forced to flee them. Thereafter, for a century and a half, there is no mention of Londinium in recorded history. The city emerged from oblivion early in the 7th century when the first St Paul's Cathedral was built during efforts to Christianize the city's intractable people.

In 851, Vikings sacked the city in what was perhaps the worst of many raids. Calm and order were restored by King Alfred and his descendants, but in 1017 the people of Lunduntown, as it was then called, had no alternative but to permit the Danish leader Canute to be crowned in their city as "King of all England".

Two cities

In 1060, the pious King Edward the Confessor took a major step in London's development by moving his court outside the walled city, a short distance upstream. He built a new palace for himself, and a minster (the forerunner of Westminster Abbey) for the monks of St Peter. Thus, in one stroke he created for ever the dichotomy between the commercial City of London and the royal and administrative precinct of Westminster.

The new abbey was consecrated just a few weeks before Edward's death. William of Normandy ("the Conqueror") rushed across the Channel with his cavalry to seize power, defeating the recently installed King Harold at the Battle of Hastings in 1066. William had himself crowned in style at the new abbey on Christmas Day the same year. To keep watch over his Anglo-Saxon subjects, he ordered construction of the Tower on the Thames bank.

London began to regain its former importance, attracting in the process a large number of immigrant merchants. By 1215, the nobles and merchant class had grown so strong that they were able to force King John to sign the

Magna Carta at Runnymede, an island in the Thames near Windsor. The document granted important rights to citizens and special privileges to the city of London, but limited the rights of the king and obliged him to accept that his will could be bound by law.

The Black Death of 1348 set things back when it destroyed half of London's population. In the ensuing social turmoil, the Peasants' Revolt of 1381 saw the city attacked by rioters demanding an end to the shilling-a-head poll tax.

Breakaway Church

The influence of the Church of Rome came to an abrupt end during the reign of Henry VIII. The break came over Henry's demand for divorce from his first wife Catherine of Aragon in order to marry Anne Boleyn. Rebuffed, Henry declared England independent, dissolved the monasteries and seized church properties. They provided him with enough funds to live up to his royal standards, seen most notably in the palace at Hampton Court.

The country experienced a golden age under his daughter, Elizabeth I. This was the era of literary figures such as Francis Bacon, Christopher Marlowe, Ben Jonson and William Shakespeare, whose plays were performed at the Globe Theatre in the rough-and-tumble borough of Southwark on the south bank of the Thames. Under Elizabeth's tutelage, English naval supremacy was established, and her fleet brought the Spanish Armada to grief in 1588. English merchants amassed huge fortunes trading with the Middle East, Russia and the East Indies.

Parliament's coup d'état

In the mid-17th century, a power struggle between Charles I and the radical Puritans of the House of Commons culminated in civil war. London City merchants took the side of Parliament, and their contributions were instrumental in defeating the Royalists. The king was beheaded in 1649, and Oliver Cromwell served as Lord Protector until his death nine years later.

The monarchy was no sooner restored, under Charles II, than two disasters struck London. The Great Plague of 1665 wiped out one-third of the population, and a year later the Great Fire raged for several days, destroying most of the rat-infested wooden houses crowded within the city walls. More than 13,000 dwellings and 87 churches were lost in the conflagration.

New face of London

For London's reconstruction, the architect Sir Christopher Wren was thwarted in his plan to endow the city some spaciousness and grandeur. He succeeded in giving London more than 50 majestic churches, but the city was rebuilt according to much the same crowded medieval street pattern—though brick and stone did at least replace timber and thatch. West of the original walled city, a 150-year building boom was just beginning. On the estates of the great landowners (today's West End), the first new developments of elegant terraces set around green squares sprang up, and London's elite began their exodus westwards.

In the 18th century, through its trade with the East and West Indies, London became one of Europe's most important commercial centres; its trade quintupled in the course of the century. It was also a brilliant cultural magnet. Literary figures such as Swift, Pope and Dr Johnson gathered in the coffee houses and Handel composed music for the royal court. But there was another side to the coin: London was now the world's largest city, and among the poor huddled in the slums east of the City (the "East End") and south of the river, alcoholism, prostitution and crime were rife.

The thriving affairs of the Empire hit a snag when rebellion broke out in the American colonies and George III was forced to let them go. As the century turned, Britain had to do battle with France as well, but the Duke of Wellington put a definitive end to Napoleon's ambitions at Waterloo.

Into the modern era

In 1802, four huge new docks began to handle the expanding international trade, augmented by the goods that Britain was churning out in the early days of the Industrial Revolution. Workers streamed into London, swelling the slums; Charles Dickens documented the appalling conditions in which they laboured and struggled to survive.

The Industrial Revolution also brought changes in the means of transport: buses, trains and the world's first underground railway meant an increase in mobility for Londoners. New communities sprouted up around the outlying underground stations, and soon they were swallowed up by an ever-expanding city.

During World War I, London was bombed by German zeppelins. But this was nothing compared to the air raids of World War II, which killed or injured

80,000 people and gutted thousands of buildings. In the post-war reconstruction, skyscrapers altered London's skyline and multi-storey dwellings replaced the sordid slums.

The face of London continues to change. The Docklands area, doomed by container shipping, has been transformed into the futuristic Canary Wharf residential and commercial development. Across the river, an ambitious project to regenerate London's largest derelict site saw a 1,400-home village built on the North Greenwich peninsula. And the 21st century got off to a dazzling start with the opening of Tate Modern, a new gallery of modern art housed in the old Bankside power station, while the award of the 2012 Olympic Games to London was a recognition of its status as one of the most vibrant, multicultural cities in the world.

KINGS OF THE ROAD

In order to receive their licence, London's black-cab drivers must first prove that they have mastered "The Knowledge". They do this by committing to memory a phenomenal 320 routes taking in 1400 landmarks and 25,000 streets within a 6-mile radius of Charing Cross, as laid out by the Public Carriage Office in its Guide to Learning the Knowledge of London. It can take up to four years to pass the test, by which time the cabbies will have acquired the coveted All-London licence and a near-mystical grasp of the capital's topography.

citySights

The City	16
The oldest part of town, occupying the site of the original Roman settlement	
West End	26
Shops and parks, museums and a dazzling nightlife	
Westminster	38
Government and royalty	
South Bank	58
Museums and arts complexes, and riverside walkway	
East End and Docklands	68
London's newest and boldest attractions	
Excursions	76
Close to the capital and further afield	

THE CITY

The unchallenged centre of Britain's financial life since its foundation as a Roman garrison town 2,000 years ago, the Square Mile pulsates with the thrill of unfettered wheeler-dealing and frenzied money-making. The excitement is contained to the weekdays, when the City's workers flood in to fill the ancient streets. Come here on Saturday or Sunday and it's as sleepy as a country village—the perfect time to explore.

The City has survived several disasters in its long history, not least the Great Fire of 1666 and the Blitz during World War II. Each time it has been rebuilt along exactly the same street plan, allowing it to be always ultra-modern architecturally, and yet retain a powerful sense of the place described by writers from Chaucer to Dickens.

THE DISTRICT AT A GLANCE

SIGHTS

Architecture
St Bride's 16
St Bartholomew's.....18
St Paul's ★ 18
St Stephen Walbrook 19
Guildhall 19
The Monument ★ 20
Tower of London ★ ...21
Tower Bridge ★ 21

Art
Guildhall Art Gallery 20

Atmosphere
Old Bailey................18

Museums
Dr Johnson's House..17
Museum of London ★ 19
Bank of England Museum 19
Clockmakers' Museum 20

WALKING TOUR 22

WINING AND DINING 88

St Bride's (F3) The printing trade first set itself up in Fleet Street during the 16th century because of its position between those twin bastions of the written word, the lawyers at the Inns of Court and the churchmen based at St Paul's. Two centuries later, the street became home to the fledgling newspaper business, from which time this fine church designed by Christopher Wren earned its nickname of the "printers' church". The printers and their newspapers have since moved away from their traditional Fleet Street location,

Bank tube station was named after the nearby Bank of England.

although you can find out more about them in a small museum based in the crypt. The church's glorious spire, 69 m (225 ft) high, is the tallest of any of Wren's creations. It's said to have been the inspiration for the traditional tiered and white-iced wedding cake—a pastry cook who lived in Fleet Street at the end of the 18th century became famous for his edible reproductions of the tiered steeple. • Daily 8am–4.45pm; Tues, Wed, Fri, music recitals at 1.15pm except during Lent, Advent and in August • Fleet Street, EC4 ⊖ Blackfriars

Dr Johnson's House (F3) A small, signposted alley on the north side of Fleet Street leads to the house where Samuel Johnson lived from 1749 to 1759. He wrote the first English dictionary in the attic, aided by six clerks. There are portraits of Johnson and his many acquaintances on display. Follow in the great man's footsteps by taking refreshment at the nearby Olde Cheshire Cheese pub, where he was a regular customer. • Mon–Sat, 11am–5.30pm; Oct–Apr until 5pm • 17 Gough Square off Hind Court, EC4 ⊖ Blackfriars/Chancery Lane

Old Bailey (Central Criminal Courts) (F3) Continue east along Fleet Street to Ludgate Hill. Before climbing up to St Paul's, turn left to find the best-known criminal courts in the world. For an intriguing insight into the workings of Britain's ancient justice system, you can sit in a public gallery and watch the barristers and judges at work. • Visitors' Gallery open to the public Mon–Fri 9.45am–1pm and 2–4pm or until courts rise. No cameras/ bags/telephones allowed. • Old Bailey and Newgate Street, EC4 ⊖ St Paul's

Priory Church of St Bartholomew the Great (F3) Located next to the famous St Bart's Hospital, just across Newgate Street from the Old Bailey, this small, hidden-away church is a rare survivor of medieval London. It was founded in 1123 by Prior Rahere, a courtier of Henry I, whose tomb lies next to the high altar. The ancient Lady Chapel, secularized during the Reformation, was once used as a printing house and counted Benjamin Franklin among its workers. • Tues–Fri 8.30am–5pm; Sat 10.30am–1.30pm; Sun 8.30am–1pm and 2.30–8pm • West Smithfield, EC1 ⊖ Farringdon/St Paul's

St Paul's Cathedral (F3) At the top of Ludgate Hill is the domed building that dominates the London skyline, the crowning achievement of England's greatest architect, Sir Christopher Wren. The cathedral is the fifth church dedicated to London's patron saint to stand on this site. When the fourth one burned down in the Great Fire of 1666, Wren found in the ashes the old centre stone inscribed with *Resurgam* (I shall rise again) and had the word carved on the south door pediment of his new cathedral. St Paul's was the scene of the state funerals of Lord Nelson and the Duke of Wellington and the wedding of Prince Charles and Lady Diana Spencer. The baroque interior looks spectacular following the renovations carried out for the cathedral's 300th anniversary in 2008, from the resplendent gilt of the nave to Grinling Gibbons's superbly carved choir stalls. Painters' Corner shelters the monuments of many great artists of the past, including Van Dyck and Constable. Go down into the crypt to view Wren's tomb, his architectural models, church vestments and other treasures. Then climb up to the Whispering Gallery to try out its acoustics, and even higher to the Stone and Golden Galleries for a superb view. • Mon–Sat 8.30am–4pm (last admission). Galleries open at 9.30am (extra charge) • Ludgate Hill, EC4 ⊖ St Paul's

Museum of London (G3) From behind St Paul's, it's worth taking a brief detour north to this museum, which presents a fascinating overview of the history of London from prehistoric days to the present. A portion of the old Roman wall is visible through a large window; you can buy a wall walk brochure to follow along the remaining bits outside the museum. An impressive audio-visual display recreates the Great Fire of London. The eclectic exhibits include the death mask of Oliver Cromwell, relics of the Great Plague, a 1940s air-raid shelter, and the Lord Mayor's 18th-century rococo state coach. A gallery devoted to medieval London opened in 2005. • Mon–Sat 10am–5.50pm, Sun from noon • 150 London Wall, EC2 ⊖ St Paul's

Bank of England Museum (G3) Weave your way back through a labyrinth of side streets to the institution which oversees the nation's financial affairs and underwrites the pound in your pocket. The Bank of England was founded in 1694 as a way of funding William III's wars with France. At this surprisingly interesting museum, the history of the bank is told with gold bars and plenty of banknotes among the props. There are some absorbing exhibits on forgery, as well as high-tech displays illustrating how the bank keeps track of the international money markets. • Mon–Fri 10am–5pm • Bartholomew Lane, EC2 ⊖ Bank

St Stephen Walbrook (G3) The exquisite parish church of the Lord Mayor of London was among the first of the churches to be rebuilt by Sir Christopher Wren after the Great Fire. The interior is extremely light and airy; beneath the wood and plaster dome is a travertine marble altar by Henry Moore (1972). The church has superb acoustics, and organ recitals are held every Friday at 12.30pm • Wed–Fri 11.30am–4.30pm • Walbrook, EC4 ⊖ Bank

Guildhall (G3) The centre of the City of London's civic government since the Middle Ages, this magnificent hall has twice risen from the ashes—it was victim of the Great Fire of 1666 and the Blitz, nearly three centuries later. It's one of England's largest public halls and major treason trials were held here, including those of Lady Jane Grey and Archbishop Cranmer. Despite its various reconstructions, the building still retains its original medieval flavour, with the banners and shields of the City's principal Livery Companies hanging beneath

Gothic-style windows. There are also monuments to Nelson, Wellington and Churchill, while the unusual statues by the West Gallery are of Gog and Magog. These giant figures represent legendary inhabitants of ancient England, and were popular features of medieval and Elizabethan pageants. • May–Sept daily 10am–5pm; rest of year closed Sun. ☎ 7606 3030 ext 1463 • Guildhall Yard, EC4 ⊖ Bank

Guildhall Art Gallery (G3) The collection of the Corporation of London consists mainly of British art from the 17th century onwards. There are portraits of various mayors and several paintings of the city itself, giving a good idea of its remarkable development over the centuries. Better-known artists on display include Constable, the pre-Raphaelite Millais and Lord Leighton. It's hard to miss John Singleton Copley's gargantuan painting, *The Defeat of the Floating Batteries at Gibraltar*—when the gallery was rebuilt after being bombed in the war, one room had to be specially designed to accommodate it. Only a fraction of the Corporation's vast collection can be shown at any one time, but the policy of rotating the paintings means there's always the chance to see something different.In the basement you can see the excavated remains of a Roman amphitheatre. • Mon–Sat 10am–5pm; Sun noon–4pm ☎ 7332 3700 or 7332 1462 • Guildhall Yard EC4 ⊖ Bank

Clockmakers' Museum (G3) The Clockmakers' Company was established by Royal Charter in 1631, so their collection of clocks, watches and other timepieces has an impressively long pedigree. The museum in the Guildhall has been revamped, but pride of place still goes to John Harrison's marine chronometer. This invention allowed the accurate calculation of longitude while at sea, giving Britain's mariners a crucial advantage over their rivals. The museum is well worth a visit—as long as you have the time. • Mon–Sat 9.30am–4.45pm • Aldermanbury EC4 ⊖ Bank

The Monument (G4) The Doric column in white Portland stone that commemorates the Great Fire of London is reached by heading south from the Bank along King William Street. Its height of 61 m (200 ft) measures the exact distance to the baker's shop on Pudding Lane where the conflagration of 1666 is popularly thought to have started. Designed by Sir Christopher Wren and

Robert Hooke in the 1670s, the column has 311 spiralling stairs which you can climb for views of the City. • Daily 9.30am–5pm ☎ 7626 2717 • Monument Street, EC3 ⊖ Monument

Tower of London (H4) Situated east along the river, the Tower ranks as one of the world's most famous buildings. Try and get there early in the day, as there's often a long queue, and avoid Sundays if you can. There's plenty to see, as the building is at once palace, fortress, prison and execution site, with several museums and the Jewel House, holding the precious Crown Jewels.

The first stones of the Tower were laid in the 11th century, when William the Conqueror wanted to defend his position as invading ruler. Now it's guarded by colourful Yeoman Warders (the famous Beefeaters), who act as humorous and lively guides, recounting the Tower's gruesome history, and pose obligingly for photographs. Among the famous prisoners of the Bloody Tower were Sir Thomas More, Anne Boleyn and Sir Walter Raleigh, all on their way to the scaffold, and it was here that Richard of Gloucester allegedly left his two prince nephews to be murdered, while he went off to be crowned Richard III.

In the Palace of Edward I, costumed attendants in candle-lit rooms evoke the 13th century. The Ceremony of the Keys has taken place every evening for the past 700 years: the Chief Warder locks the oak doors "against the mob" as bugles sound the Last Post. • Mar–Oct, Tues–Sat 9am–6pm, Sun, Mon 10am–6pm; Nov–Feb Tues–Sat 9am–5pm, Sun, Mon 10am–5pm (last admission one hour before closing); Ceremony of the Keys: 9.50pm. To attend, apply in writing well in advance to: Operations Dept., HM Tower of London, EC3N 4AB (encl. international reply coupon or stamped, addressed envelope) • Tower Hill, EC3 ⊖ Tower Hill

Tower Bridge (H4) Spanning the Thames next to the Tower is this great work of Victorian engineering, whose hefty drawbridges can open up in 90 seconds to let tall ships through. You can visit inside the bridge itself, where the Tower Bridge Exhibition recounts its history and offers a chance to venture out onto the high elevated walkways. Completed in 1894, the bridge was originally powered by steam, and you can see the pumping engines, accumulators and boilers during your visit. • Daily Apr–Sept 10am–5.30pm; Oct–Mar 9.30am–5pm • Last tour 1 hr 15 min before closing ⊖ Tower Hill

WALKING TOUR: THE CITY

One of Wren's best-known structures is a 61-m (202-ft) column that commemorates the Great Fire, known simply as the **Monument**, and just west of **Pudding Lane**. Its height measures the exact distance from Farryner's bakery. Wren collaborated with his friend, the scientist Robert Hooke, on the design and as the highest freestanding stone column in the world, it served as a powerful statement that London was back in business after the inferno.

Head northwards in the footsteps of Samuel Pepys, who on September 5 1666 recorded in his diary that he walked along **Gracechurch Street** and **Lombard Street** and found them "all in dust". Halfway along Lombard Street is **St Edmund's**, another Wren-Hooke collaboration. Note that among the decorations on the church's tower is the unexpected sight of pineapples, a fruit that had only recently been available in London and was the talk of the town.

Continue west on Lombard Street to **Cornhill**. The huge **Royal Exchange** building dates from 1844 and is now an upmarket shopping arcade; in 1666 it was the City's trading centre, and the smell of burning cinnamon and pepper stored here was said to have filled the air. Opposite it on the crossroads, **Mansion House** is the official residence of the Lord Mayor of London. On the right-hand side of this, look out for **St Stephen Walbrook**. With its fine central dome, this delightful Wren church is often considered to have been a trial run for St Paul's.

Return to Mansion House and turn left onto **Cheapside** (Chepe was the Old English word for market). On the left-hand side of this broad thoroughfare is Wren's **St Mary-le-Bow**. This boasts one of the architect's finest spires, though the church's Bow Bells are more famous, as anyone born within their sound is said to be a true cockney.

At the western end of Cheapside you arrive at **St Paul's Cathedral**, Wren's masterpiece and one of the world's most spectacular works of baroque architecture.

THE CITY

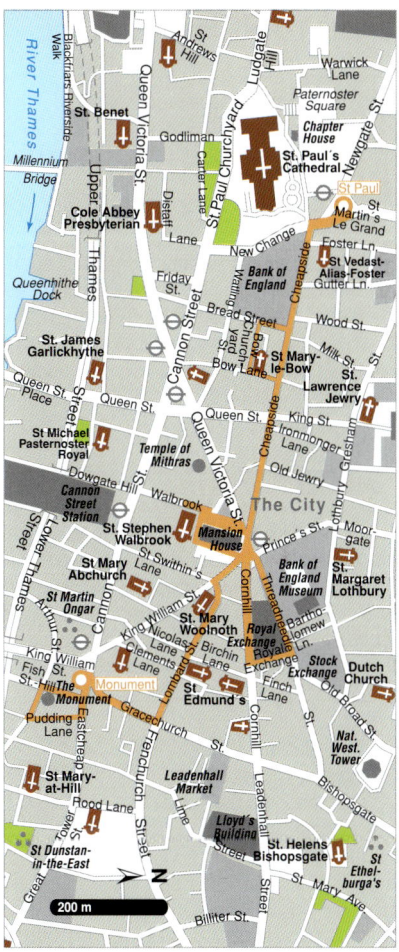

AFTER THE FIRE: WREN AND THE RECONSTRUCTION OF LONDON

The Great Fire of London began in the early hours of September 2, 1666 on Pudding Lane, at the home of Thomas Farryner, the King's baker. Within three days the conflagration had destroyed 80 per cent of the City of London, including almost 90 churches and 13,000 houses. Fortunately, the task of rebuilding the city was given to Christopher Wren, an astronomer who also turned out to be an architect of genius.

Start:
⊖ Monument

Finish:
⊖ St Paul's

BEFORE THE FLAMES: LONDON'S EARLY ARCHITECTURE

Most of London's ancient buildings had been destroyed by the time the Great Fire of 1666 had done its worst. The city we see today is largely a creation of the last three centuries. But it is still possible to find examples from earlier architectural periods.

Roman London
Boudicca trashed London in AD 62 but the city was soon rebuilt. Today the main visible sign of Roman presence is the remains of the defensive wall erected in the first part of the 2nd century. The best places to see these fortifications are in the Museum of London's garden; at St Giles Church, where you'll find a slice of the Cripplegate Bastion; and on Trinity Square on Tower Hill, which has a fragment of the wall 7 m (23 ft) high.

The route taken by some of the major roads leading in and out of the city are still governed by the original Roman layout of the capital as the hub of their nationwide road network. The Romans' trademark road design—very broad and straight as a die—can be seen in Bishopsgate, which leads out of the City north of London Bridge and once allowed Roman legionnaires to quick-march to Lincoln and York; and in Oxford Street and Notting Hill, which follow the course of the old Roman road to Silchester, west of Reading. Watling Street was once the Roman road from Dover to St Albans and followed the course of modern-day Cheapside, but its origins can best be seen in Edgware Road heading north from Marble Arch.

The medieval city
Westminster Abbey was completed under Edward the Confessor in 1066. The same year William the Conqueror immediately set about building the Tower of London from stone imported from Caen in Normandy in a style new to England, the round-arched Romanesque.

The development of medieval London was rapid. Notable examples of extant later-Norman buildings include the magnificent Westminster Hall inside the Houses of Parliament, built by William II in 1097 and with a spectacular hammerbeam roof dating from the reign of Richard II; the Gothic revamp of Westminster Abbey, carried out under Henry III in 1245; the Old Hall in Lincoln's Inn (1492), once the living room for the community of lawyers who were originally in residence here; and Eltham Palace in southeast London, with a splendid 15th-century hall.

Tudors, Stuarts and the Interregnum

The crowning glory of the Tudor period in London is west of the City at Hampton Court, built in 1514 by Cardinal Wolsey and "confiscated" by Henry VIII in 1528. At a more down-to-earth level are two 16th-century pubs in East London. The Prospect of Whitby on Wapping High Street dates from 1520 and has huge timber beams, flagstone floors and a good view over the Thames, while across the river in Rotherhithe, the Mayflower dates from 1550 and was the place where Captain Christopher Jones, master of The Mayflower, moored his ship before taking the Pilgrim Fathers to America.

A few gems of early Stuart architecture can be seen. The little-known Prince Henry's Room at 17 Fleet Street is a fine oak-panelled Jacobean house once used by the lawyers of Prince Henry, James I's eldest son, in around 1610. Far grander is the Piazza at Covent Garden, designed in 1631 by Inigo Jones, the leading architect of the day. He was also responsible for the Queen's House in Greenwich, the first Palladian villa built in England, and the marvellous Banqueting House in Whitehall. The sublime Charlton House in southeast London was completed in 1612 and is the only complete Jacobean house in the city.

The tower of All Hallows by the Tower (1658–59) is notable for being the only one in London to have had work carried out on it during Cromwell's Protectorate, and it has somehow managed to survive the Great Fire and a Luftwaffe bomb that hit the church in 1940.

WEST END

The West End is a fairly hazy geographical term for that part of London developed west of the City, and starkly distinguished by its affluence and grandeur from the poorer East End that spread out in the opposite direction towards the docks. Nowadays the name is equally suggestive of the razzmatazz of London's theatreland, upmarket restaurants and glamorous nightclubs. Also encompassed within this large area are world-class museums and art galleries, superlative shopping streets, and beautiful city parks.

THE DISTRICT AT A GLANCE

SIGHTS

Architecture
Inns of Court 26
St James's Church 31

Art
Wallace Collection ...29
Courtauld Gallery.....33
Gilbert Collection.....33

Atmosphere
Piccadilly Circus ★ 31
Leicester Square.......32

Museums
Dickens's House........27
British Museum ★ 28
Madame Tussauds ...28
Sherlock Holmes Museum...................29
London Transport Museum...................33
Theatre Museum......33

Retail Therapy
Oxford Street...........29
Marks & Spencer 30
Selfridges 30
Bond Street 30
Liberty plc................30
Carnaby Street.........30
Fortnum & Mason ...32
Covent Garden ★ 32

Greenery
Regent's Park...........28
London Zoo ★ 29

WALKING TOUR 34

WINING AND DINING 88

Inns of Court (E–F3–4) Occupying sizeable chunks of land from the Victoria Embankment to Holborn, the four inns were established in the 14th century as a way of providing lodging for lawyers and law students. They make up a network of alleys and courtyards much like the Oxford or Cambridge colleges. Inner and Middle Temples take their name from the Knights Templar who had built a church and monastery in the precinct. Magnificent 16th-century Middle Tem-

The outside tables at Covent Garden soon fill up with weary shoppers.

ple Hall is unfortunately no longer open to the public. However, you can visit the massive Victorian-Gothic Royal Courts of Justice (E 3), between Fleet Street and Chancery Lane. The gardens of Lincoln's Inn (E 3) are a haven of peace. At Lincoln's gatehouse, look for Henry VIII's coat of arms above the oak doorways. Other highlights are the linenfold panelling in Old Hall, and the chapel. Gray's Inn (E 2–3) is the place where Shakespeare's *Comedy of Errors* was first performed (1594). Its gardens were laid out by Sir Francis Bacon with catalpa cuttings brought from America by Sir Walter Raleigh. • **High Holborn, WC1** ⊖ Temple/Chancery Lane

Dickens's House (E2) Many of Dickens's devoted readers will make the pilgrimage to this house a short distance north of Gray's Inn. He had several homes in London, but this is the only one to have survived. He lived here for two years and, in his typically industrious fashion, wrote *Oliver Twist* and *Nicholas Nickleby* during that time. On display are several mementoes of the author, including the desk where he wrote his novels, totally oblivious to the commotion of family life going on around him. • Mon–Sat 10am–5pm, Sun 11am–5pm • 48 Doughty Street, WC1 ⊖ Russell Square

British Museum (D2–3) The treasures packed within London's largest and most prestigious museum include Egyptian mummies, the Elgin Marbles and the Sutton Hoo hoard, a memorial to a 7th-century Anglo-Saxon king. The Rosetta Stone, which the French looted from Egypt and subsequently lost to the British, also resides here; it was the key to deciphering Egyptian hieroglyphics. Really riveting is the leather-like 2,000-year-old body of Lindow Man found in a waterlogged peat bog. Three galleries are devoted to Mesopotamian and Anatolian treasures, including some exquisite jewellery. Surrounding the Reading Room, the newly renovated Great Court is covered by a spectacular glass roof composed of 3,312 triangular panes. The Wellcome Gallery of Ethnography opened in 2003 and contains items from Captain Cook's voyages to the South Seas and a statue from Easter Island. • **Daily 10am–5.30pm, Thurs, Fri 10am–8.30pm; Reading Room till 8.30pm Thurs, till 6pm Fri; Great Court Sun–Wed 9am–6pm, Thurs–Sat 9am–11pm** ☎ 7323 8299 • Great Russell Street, WC1 ⊖ Tottenham Court Road, Russell Square or Holborn

Madame Tussauds (B2) A brisk 20-minute walk up Gower Street and then left along Euston Road to Marylebone brings you to the famous wax museum, featuring chillingly lifelike portraits of the famous and infamous, plus a scary Chamber of Horrors. The Spirit of London ride re-creates the city over the ages with all its sounds and smells. It's worth getting a combined ticket to include the adjacent Stardome and its spectacular 360° show, The Wonderful World of Stars. • **Daily 9am–6pm** • Marylebone Road, NW1 ⊖ Baker Street

Regent's Park (B1–2) A block north lies this most elegant of city parks. Architect John Nash won the competition supported by the Prince Regent for a park and a street linking it to Westminster and it was completed in 1828. There's a lot to do here, with the Zoo, a boating lake, Queen Mary's rose garden and a summertime open-air Shakespeare theatre. Enjoy Nash's effortlessly stylish terraces of Park Crescent and Outer Circle, and the splendid Regent Street to the south, best known for Hamley's toy shop. • **Daily till dusk** ⊖ Baker Street

WEST END 29

London Zoo (off map by B1) Pick up a map at the main entrance and check on the feeding times, which always provide the best entertainment. The Web of Life organizes encounters with animals for children and puts on special shows. • Daily 10am–5.30pm; Oct–Feb till 4pm or dusk (last admission 1hr before dusk) • Regent's Park, NW1 ⊖ Camden Town or Boat transport from Camden Lock or Little Venice, buses 274, C2, Z1 (summer only)

Sherlock Holmes Museum (B2) As every fan of Sherlock Holmes knows, the world's greatest detective lived at 221b Baker Street, although in Conan Doyle's day the address didn't actually exist. The number has been appended to a different building on Baker Street, where this period reconstruction contains details such as deerstalker hat, calabash pipe and magnifying glass. Carry on up Baker Street to the tube station and you'll find a statue of the sleuth. • Daily 9.30am–6pm ☎ 7935 8866 • 221b Baker Street, NW1 ⊖ Baker Street

Wallace Collection (B3) Walk down Baker Street then turn left into Fitzharding Street to reach the impressive 18th-century house of art collector Sir Richard Wallace. It has some outstanding French paintings of the 17th and 18th centuries, Sèvres porcelain, furniture, and Frans Hals's much-loved portrait of the *Laughing Cavalier*. Have a snack in the café in the Sculpture Garden. • Daily 10am–5pm • Hertford House, Manchester Square, W1 ⊖ Bond Street

Oxford Street (B–D3) Ready for some retail therapy? Almost all roads south from Regent's Park lead

TEATIME TREATS

Teatime in the bustling city is possibly something only a tourist has time for, at least on a working day. In the proper British fashion, tea is served from around 4pm and includes a variety of sandwiches and several kinds of cakes, scones and pastries, all washed down with pots of strong tea, taken with milk, of course. Most department stores have attractive cafés, tearooms and stand-up snack bars which provide welcome respite during a shopping spree. "High tea" is a sustaining meal that may include hot dishes, meat pies, sausage rolls, cold meats and salads —just what you need after a bout of museum-visiting. It can also be a good alternative to pre-theatre dinner.

Fresh scones.

to this bustling 3-km (2-mile) shopping street. Selfridges, John Lewis, Marks and Spencer's, HMV and the Virgin Megastore are all here. At the western end you'll find Marble Arch, built by John Nash and intended as an entrance to Buckingham Palace. Unfortunately it turned out to be too small for the task and was moved here in 1851, finding a new role as a glorified traffic island. ⊖ Marble Arch/Bond Street/Oxford Circus/Tottenham Court Road

Marks & Spencer (B3) Renowned for its high quality. Men's and women's clothing, toiletries, furnishings and select foods. Other branches on Kensington High Street and Kings Road. • Mon–Fri 9am–9pm, Sat 8.30am– 7.30pm, Sun noon–6pm • 458 Oxford Street, W1 ⊖ Bond Street, Marble Arch

Selfridges (B3) Vast, comprehensive department store that offers just about everything—fine fashions, household wares, electronics and a vast food hall. • Mon–Wed 10am–7pm, Thurs, Fri 10am–8pm, Sat 9.30am–7pm, Sun noon–6pm • 400 Oxford Street, W1 ⊖ Bond Street

Bond Street (C3–4) London's most upmarket shopping street runs south from Oxford Street, though you won't see its internationally famous name on any signs as it's in fact an amalgam of two different thoroughfares, New Bond Street and Old Bond Street. It's renowned for classic haute couture, prestige jewellery shops, perfumeries and top art galleries and auction houses, such as Sotheby's. ⊖ Bond Street

Liberty plc (C3) Department store with a mock-Tudor façade, famous for its distinctive printed fabrics. • Mon–Wed 10am–6.30pm, Thurs 10am–8pm, Fri, Sat 10 am.–7pm, Sun noon–6pm • 210–220 Regent Street, W1 ⊖ Oxford Circus

Carnaby Street (C3–4) Tucked away behind Regent Street south of Oxford Circus, Carnaby Street was the flashy face of London's Swinging Sixties era. Once the party was over, the trendy boutiques gave way to tacky souvenir shops trading on the iconic status of the street's name. Things have improved lately, and cutting-edge fashion houses are once again moving into the area. ⊖ Oxford Circus

The bright lights of Piccadilly, named for a frilly collar called a piccadil.

Piccadilly Circus (D4) If London can be said to have a centre, this is probably the best candidate. Lying at the confluence of Regent Street, Shaftesbury Avenue and Piccadilly, it's the city's glitziest, neon-lit spot. The landmark statue of Eros actually has nothing to do with the god of love, and is properly called the Angel of Christian Charity, dedicated to the Victorian philanthropist, Lord Shaftesbury. ⊖ Piccadilly Circus

St James's Church (D4) Nearby on Piccadilly is the last of the London churches designed by Wren, and reputedly the one he liked best. Note the wood carving by Grinling Gibbons festooning the organ case, the font and the altarpiece. The visionary poet and artist William Blake was baptised in the church in 1757. Many non-ecclesiastical activities take place here: a crafts market on Friday and Saturday, wholefood café, brass-rubbing centre and lunchtime concerts Monday and Friday. • **Open daily 8am–7pm** • Piccadilly, W1 ⊖ Piccadilly Circus

Leicester Square (D4) East of Piccadilly Circus is another of the city's great hangouts, a large, mainly pedestrianized space that contains some of London's biggest cinemas. It's also a convenient starting point for exploring Chinatown, based around Gerrard Street, and the Soho district, with its atmospheric cafés, restaurants and clubs of every persuasion. ⊖ Leicester Square

Fortnum & Mason (C4) The firm was founded in 1707 by William Fortnum, one of Queen Anne's footmen. The sales clerks still glide over the red carpets in formal morning dress. A good place to shop for exotic comestible gifts, beautifully packaged in jars, cans, canisters and fabulous hampers. Non-edibles too, like porcelain and crystal, and an elegant tea room. • Mon–Sat 10am–6.30pm • 181 Piccadilly, W1 ⊖ Green Park

Covent Garden (E4) Carry on eastwards across Charing Cross Road to where, in place of the old Covent Garden vegetable and flower market celebrated by Fielding and Hogarth, you'll find a fashionable array of boutiques and stalls sell-

MIND THE GAP

Travelling on the Tube, you'll soon notice the public announcement "Mind the Gap", repeated hypnotically every time the train pulls in at stations where there's a significant distance between the straight-sided carriage and the curving platform (first built to follow the course of the main roads up above). The biggest gaps are at Piccadilly Circus, Waterloo and Bank, on the Central Line. The phrase has now passed into popular culture, appearing on T-shirts, mugs and wall posters. It has featured in movies, poems, pop songs and video games, and is the title of a modern classical composition for cello and orchestra by Robert Steadman, which, inevitably, begins and ends with the performers calling out "Mind the Gap".

ing antiques, clothing and crafts. They spill over into Jubilee Market south of the piazza. All around it are lively but pricey restaurants and cafés, with daily entertainment by street musicians, jugglers and performance artists. • **Covent Garden, WC2** 🚇 Covent Garden

London's Transport Museum (E4) Its smart new galleries are devoted to the history of public transport in London and its future developments, alongside old favourites such as vintage buses, trams and underground trains. The museum shop is across the way in Covent Garden Market and sells fabulous posters and other London Transport memorabilia. • **Undergoing renovation, due to re-open autumn 2007** • **Piazza, Covent Garden, WC2** 🚇 Covent Garden

Theatre Museum (E4) The British stage and its stars from Shakespeare to the present. Collections range from ancient playbills to Victorian marionettes and the costumes for Diaghilev's *Ballets Russes*. • **Tues–Sun 10am–6pm (last admission 5.30pm)** • **Russell Street, Covent Garden, WC2** 🚇 Covent Garden

Courtauld Gallery (E4) On the river side of the Strand is Somerset House, a magnificent building dating from 1776. It was originally used for governmental offices but has been renovated to house in the north wing a fine art gallery made up largely of contributions from private patrons. At its core is a splendid collection of Impressionist paintings put together by the textile tycoon Samuel Courtauld. Among the famous works hanging here are Edouard Manet's *Bar at the Folies-Bergère* and Van Gogh's *Self-Portrait with Bandaged Ear*, together with numerous paintings by Degas, Renoir, Gauguin and Cézanne. There are earlier masterpieces by Botticelli, Rubens, Dürer and Rembrandt, too. • **Daily 10am–6pm (last admission 5.15pm); Mon free entry 10am–2pm** • **Somerset House, The Strand, WC2** 🚇 Covent Garden/Temple

Gilbert Collection (E4) In the rejuvenated south building of Somerset House, this museum displays a fabulous private collection of European silver, gold snuffboxes and splendid Italian mosaics from the 16th–19th centuries. Have a drink out on the terrace overlooking the Thames. • **Mon–Sun 10am–6pm (last admission 5.20pm); free entry from 4.30pm** • **Somerset House, The Strand, WC2** 🚇 Covent Garden/Temple

WALKING TOUR: WEST END

Head along **Leicester Place**, which leads off from the northeast corner of the square. On the right-hand side is **Notre Dame de France**, with murals by Jean Cocteau. Turn left onto Lisle Street and then right onto **Wardour Street**. This is the home of the British film and television industry, while no. 90 was once occupied by the legendary Marquee club and saw the earliest gigs of such rock luminaries as Jimi Hendrix and Pink Floyd.

To the right off Wardour Street is **Gerrard Street**. The huge red oriental gates at either end, along with the pagoda-shaped telephone boxes and plethora of Chinese restaurants, indicate that this is the focal point of London's **Chinatown**. Carry on along Wardour Street across **Shaftesbury Avenue**—which alone has six magnificent Victorian-era theatre houses—and plunge into the tangle of narrow roads at the heart of Soho. The spirit of the district is epitomized by **Old Compton Street**, a right turn off Wardour Street. Packed with chic boutiques, trendy clubs, gay bars and fashionable cafés and restaurants, this buzzes with life late into the night.

Old Compton Street crosses some of Soho's liveliest thoroughfares. You can detour right onto **Dean Street**, where Karl Marx lived at no. 28 and the 7-year-old Mozart performed at no. 21, and stop for a drink at the **French House**. This pub is where Charles de Gaulle and his Free French colleagues met during World War II and the poet Dylan Thomas used to consume alcohol in epic quantities. Carry on a block to **Frith Street**. Past residents include Mozart at no.18 and John Logie Baird, the inventor of television, at no. 22; he gave the first public demonstration of television in his attic room here in 1924. Below Baird's former home is a modern Soho legend, the **Bar Italia**, open 24 hours a day (except Sundays) and a magnet for all manner of local life. Ronnie Scott's equally famous jazz club is at no. 47.

From Frith Street continue north through leafy **Soho Square** to Oxford Street. Tottenham Court Road underground station is a short distance to the right.

WEST END 35

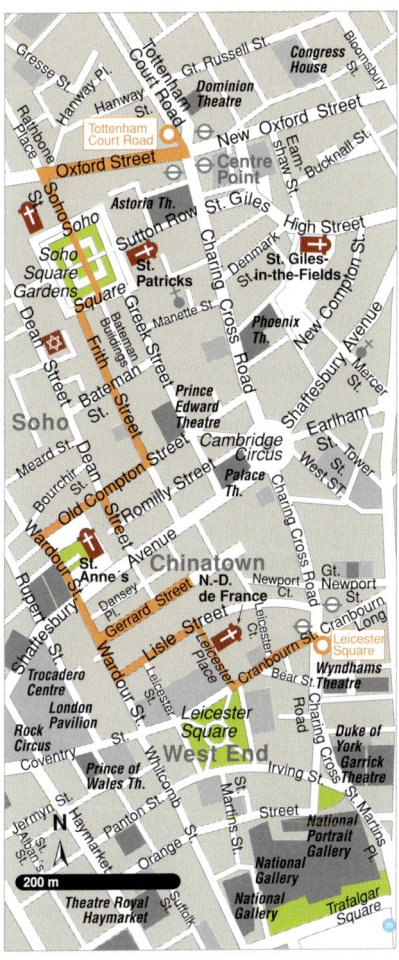

SOHO

Leicester Square was one of London's most exclusive addresses until the 19th century, when it became as rumbustious, bohemian and downright seedy as the rest of Soho and the toffs moved out. These days it's a popular meeting place and hangout for tourists and, as befits the central point of London's theatreland, the place to buy half price theatre tickets for on-the-day performances.

Start:
⊖ Leicester Square

Finish:
⊖ Tottenham Court Road

CHILDREN'S LONDON

Happily, there's no shortage of great things on offer to delight younger visitors to the capital, from imaginative and educationally stimulating museums to noisy and joyfully escapist theme parks.

Animal magic

A surefire crowd pleaser is **London Zoo** in Regent's Park: kids love the walk-through squirrel monkey area, while feeding time is a perennial hit with them: check out which beasts are being fed at what times by calling the zoo before you go (020 7722 3333).

Seriously entertaining

For high-tech, hands-on fun, the **Science Museum** in South Kensington can't be beaten. The displays on everything from electricity and medicine to cars and aeroplanes are a marvellous way to introduce children to the excitement of science as it affects their daily lives. The **Natural History Museum** next door is packed with dinosaur skeletons, has a truly itch-inducing Creepy Crawlies zone, and allows kids to experience an earthquake in the Earth Galleries section.

The enormous space of the former Bankside power station's Turbine Hall at the **Tate Modern** will take their breath away, while the many of the works on display are offbeat, quirky and downright weird. The gallery has imaginative art trails, encouraging children to follow a route around the exhibition halls and draw their own versions of selected works and styles as they go, equipped with art materials supplied by Tate Modern.

The dark side
London's grim and sometimes gruesome past serves up plenty of opportunities for children to revel in tales of horror. The **London Dungeon**, located in the dank arches of London Bridge, and the **Clink Prison Museum**, on the site of the original "Clink" gaol on Bankside, focus on the gorier side of medieval London life. But the best-known spot for contemplating treason and torture is the **Tower of London**, where red-coated Yeomen Warders known as Beefeaters take you on free tours of the castle and explain what happened to the unfortunate people who entered through Traitor's Gate.

Southbank adventure
The rays, sharks, jellyfish and piranhas at the **London Aquarium** are pretty scary, especially when viewed in startling close-up through a huge floor-to-ceiling glass wall. A stone's throw from here is the **British Airways London Eye**, probably the most spectacular observation wheel any kid will ride on. The views of the capital are unforgettable, and they'll even get the chance to see into the gardens at Buckingham Palace from it.

Fun in the park
Hyde Park provides all the space any child could want for running around and letting off steam. The adjacent **Kensington Gardens** was where JM Barrie first thought up the story of *Peter Pan*, and a superb bronze statue of the boy who never grew up can be found close to the Serpentine. At the Notting Hill end of Kensington Gardens, the **Diana, Princess of Wales Memorial Playground** has a Captain Hook-style pirate ship.

Beyond the centre
If they have any energy left after this, there's always **Chessington World of Adventures** on the outskirts of south London. This theme park has rides aimed at families with younger children, with 90 per cent of the attractions suitable for the under-twelves. Train to Chessington South and then bus 71.

WESTMINSTER

Ever since Edward the Confessor ordered his palace and Minster in the West to be built here nearly 1,000 years ago, this area has kept a firm grasp on the reins of power. These days, the Prime Minister at home at 10, Downing Street is a neighbour of the British royal family, in their London pad over at Buckingham Palace. Meanwhile, the engines of government roll on in the huge Whitehall department buildings and the magnificent Houses of Parliament. The political mix is leavened by world-class art galleries, fine architecture and close proximity to the various delights of Hyde Park, Harrods and the Chelsea Flower Show.

THE DISTRICT AT A GLANCE

SIGHTS

Architecture
St Martin-in-the-Fields 40
Banqueting House★ 41
Houses of Parliament★ 42
Westminster Abbey★ 42
St James's Palace 43
Clarence House 45
Buckingham Palace★ 46
Wellington Arch 47

Art
National Gallery★ 40
National Portrait Gallery★ 40
Tate Britain 43
Saatchi Gallery 52

Atmosphere
Trafalgar Square★ 39
Whitehall 40
10 Downing Street...41
King's Road 52

Browsing
Notting Hill 51

Museums
Cabinet War Rooms .42
Spencer House 45
Wellington Museum.46
Kensington Palace....50
V&A★ 51
Science Museum★ ...52
Natural History Museum★ 52

Chelsea Royal Hospital 53

Retail Therapy
Knightsbridge 51
Harrods 51

Greenery
St James's Park 43
Hyde Park★ 50
Kensington Gardens 50
Chelsea Physic Garden 53
Battersea Park 53

WALKING TOUR 54

WINING AND DINING 90

WESTMINSTER 39

A wind-blown flotilla of miniature boats on the pond in Hyde Park.

Trafalgar Square (D4) At the top of Whitehall is London's grandest square, known for the statue of Lord Nelson, who surveys the scene from his 51-m-high (167-ft) column. The square is named for the Battle of Trafalgar in 1805, at which Napoleon's navy was defeated but Nelson killed. The friezes at the base of the column were made from captured French cannon; the mighty lions guarding the column are the work of Sir Edward Landseer. Soon after the square was laid out, it became a tradition for political meetings and demonstrations to take place here. In the Christmas season, a large tree is set up in the centre of the square, an annual gift from Norway, and festooned with white lights, around which carol singers perform nightly. And as the bells ring out the New Year, what seems like the whole of London gathers around the fountains. The huge and famous colony of 40,000 pigeons has disappeared since the sale of birdseed was prohibited in 2000 and the mayor, Ken Livingstone, enacted by-laws to ban the feeding of pigeons within the square. ⊖ Leicester Square/Charing Cross

St Martin-in-the-Fields (D4) The lovely spire of this classical temple-style church rises over Trafalgar Square, a little taller even than Nelson's Column. Designed by James Gibbs and completed in 1726, the church has a long and honourable tradition as a refuge of the homeless. • **Closed Sun except for services; free concerts Mon, Tues, Fri 1.05pm** • Trafalgar Square, WC2 ⊖ Leicester Square/Charing Cross

National Gallery (D4) In a large neoclassical building overlooking the square, the gallery houses collections of some of the greatest European artists. Leonardo da Vinci's *Virgin of the Rocks*, Holbein's *The Ambassadors,* Rembrandt's young and old self-portraits, Turner's *Rain, Steam and Speed* and masterpieces by artists from Vermeer and Velázquez to Van Gogh are only a suggestion of the multitude of treasures that this museum houses. The helpful Micro Gallery is a catalogue on computer; enter the name of the artists whose works you want to see, and it will print out a map showing exactly where to find them. • **Daily 10am–6pm, Wed till 9pm** • Trafalgar Square, WC2 ⊖ Leicester Square/Charing Cross

National Portrait Gallery (D4) This gallery dedicated to famous British faces through the ages is located behind the National Gallery, and has what is claimed to be the only authentic portrait of Shakespeare, as well as paintings of the Brontë sisters by their brother Branwell, Henry VIII, Princess Diana, Lady Thatcher and many more. The Balcony Gallery shows some of the NPG's more recent acquisitions, and there's a rooftop restaurant. • **Sat–Wed 10am–6pm, Thurs, Fri 10am–9pm** • St Martin's Place, WC2 ⊖ Leicester Square/Charing Cross

Whitehall (D4–5) Running between Trafalgar Square and Parliament Square, this wide avenue has become a byword for government bureaucracy. It was from here that the Civil Service ran the affairs of Britain's world-wide empire in the 19th century, though its dominant role in a devolving British state is increasingly under threat. On the right-hand side of the street as you walk down Whitehall, the photogenic Household Cavalry stands watch at the Horse Guards building—the Changing of the Guard takes place each day at 11am Further along is the Cenotaph, an austere memorial designed by Edward Lutyens after

World War I to honour the dead, and the national focus of the Remembrance Sunday ceremony in November. ⊖ Charing Cross/Westminster

Banqueting House (D5) Until 1698, when it burnt down, the left (Thames) side of Whitehall was home to the vast Whitehall Palace, the London residence of the Tudor and Stuart monarchs. The palace was originally built by Cardinal Wolsey, who was turned out of his home by Henry VIII when the cardinal failed to persuade the pope to grant the king a divorce. All that survives of it today is the Banqueting House, built between 1619 and 1622 by Inigo Jones as an addition to the palace, and the first Palladian-style building in England. The hall was used for a variety of court ceremonies. Its ceiling is covered by nine large pictures commissioned by Charles I from Peter Paul Rubens, who was rewarded with a knighthood. The paintings served to glorify the Stuart dynasty, and so it is not without some irony that in 1649 Charles was taken from this very room to be beheaded on a scaffold outside the house. A scale model of the grandiose Whitehall Palace is displayed in the Museum of London. • Mon–Sat 10am–5pm (last admission 4.30pm); closed to the public during government functions • Whitehall, SW1 ⊖ Charing Cross/Westminster

10 Downing Street (D5) The official residence of every British prime minister since 1732 is situated along a small side road on the right-hand side of Whitehall. Margaret Thatcher holds the occupancy record for 20th-century PMs, and she was also the one who put up the iron gates that prevent the

CHARING CROSS

At the junction of the Strand and Whitehall, Charing was once a small hamlet whose name derived from the Old English word meaning "to turn", as this was where the road to Bath turned direction to follow the riverbank. The Cross was added later, after it became the last resting place in 1290 of the funeral cortege of Queen Eleanor, wife of Edward I, before arriving at Westminster Abbey. Edward had crosses erected on each of the cortege's 12 stops. The cross at Charing originally stood on the site now occupied by the statue of Charles I but was destroyed by Parliament in a fit of anti-Royalist pique in 1647. A replica dating from 1863 can be seen in the forecourt of Charing Cross Station.

public from wandering past the famous black door of Number 10. The Chancellor of the Exchequer occupies Number 11. • **Downing Street, SW1** ⊖ Westminster

Cabinet War Rooms (D5) In the next street along from Downing Street are the basement rooms where Sir Winston Churchill and the War Cabinet operated during World War II. They are furnished as though the great man were still here, about to launch into one of his famous morale-boosting speeches. • **Daily 9.30am–6pm • Clive Steps, King Charles Street, SW1** ⊖ Westminster

Houses of Parliament (D5) Charles Barry's stunning Victorian neo-Gothic building overlooks Parliament Square at the bottom of Whitehall. Edward the Confessor built the first Palace of Westminster on this site in 1049 and moved the royal court here from the City. After his death, William the Conqueror took it over. It remained the principal residence of the English kings for 400 years until Henry VIII acquired the Palace of Whitehall as his London home. Westminster remained nonetheless the administrative centre of the kingdom. Westminster Hall, dating from 1099, is the oldest surviving part of the Palace; most of the remainder succumbed to fire in 1834. The House of Lords and House of Commons sit here today. The Queen presides yearly over the State Opening of Parliament from the House of Lords, but no monarch is allowed admittance to the House of Commons. For entrance to the Strangers' Gallery of the House of Commons when it's in session, you have to join the queue at St Stephen's porch. The Prime Minister's Question Time draws the biggest crowds. • **House of Commons: Strangers' Gallery open to public when the House is sitting, Mon 2.30pm till House goes up; Tues–Thurs 11.30am till House goes up; Fri 9.30am–2.30pm; Prime Minister's Question Time, Wed noon–12.30pm • Apply to your embassy for a Card of Introduction.** ☎ 7219 4272 for information • To visit the House of Lords, apply to your embassy. ☎ 7219 3107 for information • **Parliament Square, SW1** ⊖ Westminster

Westminster Abbey (D5) Opposite the Houses of Parliament, this English Gothic jewel is the setting for Britain's ceremonial events—coronations (the first was that of William the Conqueror in 1066), funerals of statesmen and royalty, and royal weddings. Coronations make use of the Coronation Chair, an old oaken throne, at the High Altar. The abbey is the last resting place of many kings and queens, as well as other famous people, notably in Poets' Corner. A fine monument to the composer Handel shows him holding the pages of his Messiah. The simple tomb of Edward the Confessor, the church's founder, lies in the heart of the abbey. The Henry VII Chapel has a lovely fan-vaulted ceiling setting the scene for the Renaissance-style royal tombs of Henry and his mother Lady Margaret Beaufort. They are joined by Elizabeth I and her half-sister Mary. It is worth attending a service to hear the choristers of the Westminster school. Times are given on a noticeboard outside. • Mon, Tues, Thurs–Sat 9.30am–3.45pm, Wed 9.30am–7pm; last entry at the latest 1 hour before the door closes. ☎ 7222 2152 for information • Parliament Square, SW1 ⊖ Westminster

Tate Britain (off map by D6) A slight detour south along the river brings you to this museum founded at the end of the 19th century by the sugar millionaire, Sir Henry Tate. The collections of the venerable Tate have been spread over two galleries: Tate Britain (formerly called the Tate Gallery) is at the original site and shows the best of British painting and sculpture from the 16th century to the present day, including works by William Blake, Turner, Constable and Francis Bacon. It is linked to Tate Modern, its sister gallery on the South Bank, by a shuttle bus and boat service, as well as bicycle and pedestrian routes. • Daily 10am–5.50pm • Millbank, SW1 ⊖ Pimlico

St James's Park (D5) Head back up to Parliament Square and follow Great George Street to the oldest, and probably prettiest, of the royal parks. Originally a marshy field where women lepers from the nearby hospice kept pigs, it was drained by Henry VIII, who used to come here to hunt or to play bowls. The park was extended by Charles II, who commissioned André Le Nôtre, landscape gardener of Versailles, to do the work. Exotic wildfowl have staked their claim to the island in the lake, and the bridge offers great views of Buckingham Palace. ⊖ Green Park/St James's Park

St James's Palace (C5) Henry VIII had this red brick palace northwest of the park built on the site of St James's Hospital. For 300 years it remained one of the main residences of the English monarchs. Today, several members of the

royal family have their apartments in the palace. It was the home of Prince Charles until he moved to Clarence House in 2003 after the death of the Queen Mother. The palace is connected by an underground passage to the royal pew in the Queen's Chapel designed by Inigo Jones; the general public can attend services on Sunday morning here or at Chapel Royal in the palace precincts. The Old Guard leaves St James's Palace daily (alternate days August to March) at about 11.10am to march up the Mall to Buckingham Palace for the ceremony of the Changing of the Guard. • **Pall Mall, SW1** ⊖ Green Park

Clarence House (C5) Located quite close to St James's Palace, the former residence of the Queen Mother, who lived there from 1953 to her death in 2002, now belongs to Prince Charles. He had the 19th-century neoclassical building restored from top to bottom, and furnished the uppermost apartments for himself, his sons and his wife Camilla Parker-Bowles. The ground floor of the house is open to the public on certain occasions. • **The Mall, SW1** ☎ 7766 73 03 for information ⊖ Green Park

Spencer House (C4) At the edge of nearby Green Park is this exquisite Palladian-style palace, built by Princess Diana's ancestor, the first Earl Spencer, in the mid-18th century. The house was leased in 1985 to one of the Rothschild companies, which has painstakingly restored it and opened it as a museum (in nine antique-filled State Rooms) and art gallery. If you have a small fortune at your disposal, you can rent the premises to throw a party.

◀ *You don't have to go far to get away from the traffic and the City buzz.*

Sun 10.30am– 5.30pm; closed January and August; last admission 4.45pm; children under 10 not admitted • 27 St James's Place, SW1 ⊖ Green Park

Buckingham Palace (C5) George III must have felt that St James's Palace was getting a bit run-down and cramped, so he persuaded the Duke of Buckingham to sell him the fine house he'd had constructed not far away on the other side of Green Park. His son, George IV, had even grander ideas, and on ascending the throne hired John Nash to improve the residence. It was still unfinished on his death, and Queen Victoria was the first to benefit from the luxurious new premises. Originally, Nash designed a U-shaped palace, with a marble arch marking the entrance to the courtyard. In 1851, a fourth side was added to the palace, and the marble arch was moved to the top of Park Lane. Of the 600 rooms in "Buck House", as it's familiarly known, the Queen and her consort occupy a mere dozen, upstairs in the north wing that overlooks Green Park. Some of the royal relations also have lodgings in the palace, and the rest of the rooms are used as ceremonial lounges, staff offices and domestic quarters. Sorry, the Queen is hardly likely to invite you in for a cup of tea, but you can have a look around 18 of her ceremonial rooms, all adorned with masterpieces, including the Throne Room and the State Dining Room. These were opened to the public after Windsor Castle was severely damaged by fire, with the intention of using the proceeds to pay for the repairs. You can also see the Queen's horses and ceremonial coaches in the Royal Mews (C 6). The Queen's Gallery displays items from the royal collection in rotating exhibitions. At 11.30am in summer (with some exceptions, and weather permitting), the colourful pageant of the Changing of the Guard takes place in the forecourt of the Palace. The Old Guard from St James's Palace marches up the Mall to join the Old Guard at Buckingham Palace, and the New Guard arrives from Wellington Barracks via Birdcage Walk. • Ceremonial rooms: Aug and Sept daily 9.30am–4.15pm ☎ 7321 2233 for information. Royal Mews: March–July and October daily 11am–1.15pm; August and September daily 10am–4.15pm; Queen's Gallery daily 10am–4.30pm ☎ 7839 1377 for information on exhibitions • St James's Park, SW1 ⊖ Green Park

Wellington Museum (Apsley House) (B5) At the top of Constitution Hill, which runs along the north side of Buckingham Palace up to Hyde Park Corner,

WESTMINSTER 47

Many old shops proudly display their royal warrants, even long after their royal patron has left this world.

this is the home of the first Duke of Wellington, and was once known quite simply as "No. 1, London". The Iron Duke's remarkable collection of paintings includes works by Rubens, Velázquez, Breughel, Van Dyck, Goya and others, and you can see the Waterloo Vase presented to the duke upon his famous victory. In one of the rooms, immense gilt mirrors slide back to reveal a view over Hyde Park. • **Tues–Sun 11am–5pm** • **149 Piccadilly, W1** ⊖ **Hyde Park Corner**

Wellington Arch (B5) Designed by Decimus Burton, this Corinthian-style structure dates from 1828 and commemorates the Iron Duke's triumph over Napoleon. It originally stood at the top of Constitution Hill and served as the north gate of Buckingham Palace, with a disproportionately huge statue of Wellington on top. It was moved to Hyde Park Corner in 1882, and lost its statue. In 1912 the arch was adorned with Adrian Jones's magnificent quadriga— a four-horse chariot driven by a small boy and bearing the winged figure of peace. For a while, the arch housed London's smallest police station. In 1999 it

SHOPPER'S LONDON

London is one of the world's great shopping cities, a vast Aladdin's cave of the latest in everything from fashion and furnishings to art and the arcane. The biggest and best of the department stores are to be found on Oxford Street and in upmarket Knightsbridge. For those keen on more specialist designer clothes shops, a walk along Old Bond Street, New Bond Street or Sloane Street, off Sloane Square, should set pulses racing and credit cards running for cover.

Quirkier fashion stores are clustered around Covent Garden, while Carnaby Street has enjoyed a renaissance as a magnet for cool, offbeat boutiques. For classic English-style tailoring, Jermyn Street and Savile Row, near Piccadilly, have become bywords for sophistication and class. Expensive designer clothes demand top-end jewellery to match: the jewellers on New Bond Street and around Hatton Garden, near Farringdon, have a magnificent array of pieces on offer.

If you prefer the less expensive option of browsing in bookshops, the numerous stores along Charing Cross Road will keep you entertained for days. The lowest-priced electrical goods in London are to be found on Tottenham Court Road, while for music that avoids the mainstream, head for Soho.

Department stores

Harrods of Knightsbridge is the grande dame of luxury department stores, a place where tradition is respected and the service impeccable. Neighbouring **Harvey Nichols** sells a range of upscale cosmetics, clothes, bags and shoes, and is wildly popular with the affluent and the aspirational. Oxford Street is home to the stalwarts of the department store scene. **Marks and Spencer**'s flagship branch is at no. 458, with a range of clothes, foodstuffs, furnishings and, of course, the coveted underwear for which they are still famous. Further along at no. 400, **Selfridge's** contains a comprehensive collection of top-quality fashion accessories, designer-label clothing, lingerie and perfumes. **John Lewis**, at 278–306 Oxford Street, is legendary for its household goods, from furniture and kitchenware to Middle-Eastern carpets.

Designer fashion

Leading designers such as **Alexander McQueen** (4-5 Old Bond Street, W1), **Ozwald Boateng** (9 Vigo Street, Mayfair), **Katharine Hamnett** (20 Sloane Street, SW1) and **Nicole Fahri** (158 New Bond Street, W1) are at the cutting edge of creative flair and innovation. Boutiques like **Koh Samui** in Covent Garden and **Browns** on South Molton Street boast a staggering range of designer labels from around the world.

Specialist shops

Foyles, a bookseller of dizzying dimensions, is located on Charing Cross Road; **Asprey** of New Bond Street, jeweller to the upper-crust; **Hamleys**, on Regent Street, self-proclaimed biggest toyshop in the world; **Fortnum & Mason** on Piccadilly, for posh English tea and other foodstuffs. Even more specialized: **Anya Hindmarch**, Pont Street SW1, for luxury handbags, or **Rigby & Peller** for bespoke bras, by Royal Appointment.

passed into the care of English Heritage, and it has since been restored and adapted for public access with viewing platforms and exhibition spaces.
• April–Sept, Wed–Sun 10am–5pm; Oct–Mar, Wed–Sun 10am–4pm ☎ 7930 2726 • Hyde Park Corner ⊖ Hyde Park Corner

Hyde Park (A–B4–5) This delightful park became Henry VIII's hunting grounds after he seized the land from the monks of Westminster Abbey at the dissolution of the monasteries. Today there's boating and swimming in the Serpentine, horse-riding on Rotten Row, an informal ball game or simply sunbathing on the grass. On Sundays, at Speaker's Corner, the Marble Arch corner of the park, advocates of every cause imaginable climb onto their soapbox and declaim to the crowds gathered around—a remaining vestige of the British tradition of free speech. ⊖ Marble Arch/Hyde Park/Corner/Knightsbridge

Kensington Gardens (map 4 A5) On the west side of the Serpentine, these formal gardens were originally laid out by William III. There's a pretty sunken garden, a lily pond, an orangery and flowerbeds. Beyond, open parkland merges into Hyde Park, with features such as the Round Pond (where weekend model yacht sailing makes a good show for children), the Italian Garden fountains and the marvellously ornate Albert Memorial. The Serpentine Art Gallery shows works at the cutting edge of modern art. ⊖ High Street Kensington

Kensington Palace Situated at the western edge of Kensington Gardens is this fine Jacobean house, transformed into a palace under William III, who was fortunate enough to have builders such as Christopher Wren and Nicholas Hawksmoor on hand to do the job. The State Apartments are furnished in Stuart- and Hanoverian-era objects, highlighted by a collection of court dress and works of art belonging to the Queen. Temporary exhibitions are organized. Some of the royal relations have apartments in the palace—it was the last home of Princess Diana. There's also a tea-room in the Orangery and delightful gardens. • Daily 10am–5pm • Kensington Gardens, W8 ⊖ Queensway/High Street Kensington

Notting Hill Just northwest of the palace, the resolutely trendy Notting Hill district is home to style-conscious Londoners, and has bars and restaurants to match. It is also home to one of the longest and best-known street markets in the country: Portobello Road market has been trading since the 18th century. These days anything and everything is on sale on Friday, while there are antiques galore on Saturday. Antique shops are clustered all around the area and open throughout the week. On the last Sunday and Monday of August, the district is taken over by the famous Notting Hill Carnival. With processions, music, Caribbean food stalls and seething crowds with up to 1 million visitors, it's the biggest street party in Europe. ⊖ **Notting Hill**

Knightsbridge (B5) Located on the south side of Hyde Park, Knightsbridge is London's classiest shopping district, boasting all the big names in international fashion, top-notch restaurants and, on Brompton Road, Harrods, one of the poshest department stores on earth. ⊖ **Knightsbridge**

Harrods (A6) Its 300 departments on five floors cover 2 acres. Everything you could possibly want to buy will be found here, and the services on offer can take you from your christening to your funeral. Don't miss the fabulous food halls, walled with decorate tiles, each section introduced by a painterly display of fresh produce—even if the prices leave you feeling giddy, there's no other food store quite like this, anywhere in the world. • Mon–Sat 10am–7pm • Brompton Road, SW1 ⊖ **Knightsbridge**

Victoria and Albert Museum (V&A) (A6) Continue along Brompton Road and you will soon see the great neo-Gothic façade of the V&A. This museum of decorative arts, one of the largest in the world, was the brainchild of Prince Albert, and its origins go back to the Great Exhibition of 1851. Doll's houses, dress collections, ceramics, furniture, jewellery, and the largest collection of Indian art outside India all find their place. There are splendid galleries of silverware, and it is worth seeking out the famous Raphael cartoons—his designs for tapestries to adorn Rome's Sistine Chapel. The fabulous Glass Gallery displays more than 6,000 objects tracing 4,000 years of glassmaking. The museum shop is particularly attractive, with a good selection of books and gifts.
• **Daily 10am–5.45pm, Wed and last Fri in month 10am–10pm (only selected galleries are open in the evening); free admission** • Cromwell Road, SW7 ⊖ **South Kensington**

Science Museum (A6) Across from the V&A are two more large museums with their roots in Britain's Victorian heyday. The Science Museum is one of the most popular in London, a hands-on, visitor-friendly experience, full of old engines, veteran cars and interactive displays. It boasts a full-size replica of the Apollo 11 Lunar Lande and explains the invention of the plastic bag, has a 5-storey IMAX cinema and an Energy Exhibition that will keep you on your toes. Among the unusual exhibits in the History of Medicine rooms are Napoleon's toothbrush and Florence Nightingale's moccasins. • **Daily 10am–6pm; free admission** • Exhibition Road, SW7 ⊖ South Kensington

Natural History Museum (A6) Next door to the Science Museum is this venerable institution, which opened in 1881 and reflects the rapid impact that Darwin's theories had on the Victorian mind. Indeed, the new Darwin Centre holds a mind-boggling 22 million exhibits including the first recorded examples of many species. There are plenty of dinosaur skeletons, plus exhibits on ecology, geology and biology. Computer games, videos, interactive displays and an earthquake simulator enliven the didactic message. Everyone's heard of the extinct dodo bird, but what did it look like? The reconstruction in the Bird Gallery provides the answer. There's also an elegant new restaurant and you'll find good educational gifts in the shop. • **Mon–Sat 10am–5.50pm, Sun from 11am; free admission** • Cromwell Road, SW7 ⊖ South Kensington

King's Road (map 4, A8–B7) The backbone of London's famous Chelsea is due south of the museum area. The king referred to in the name is Charles II, during whose reign it became a fashionable hangout for the city's beau monde. This status has pretty much remained intact; in the 19th century, local residents included artists and literati Turner, Rossetti, Henry James and Oscar Wilde. Later, it was the glamorous heart of the Swinging Sixties era, and even managed to be at the centre of 1970s punk fashion, when Vivienne Westwood and Malcolm McLaren opened their notorious boutique, Sex, at no. 430. Take a walk here today and you'll still be able to get the best idea of what London's most glamorous set are up to. ⊖ Sloane Square/South Kensington

Saatchi Gallery (map 4, B7) Controversial works by modern British artists such as Damien Hirst and Tracey Emin are displayed in new premises opening in November 2007. • For details see www.saatchi-gallery.co.uk ☎ 7823 2363 • Duke of York's Building, Kings Road, SE1 ⊖ Sloane Square

Chelsea Royal Hospital (map 4, B8) Turn off King's Road at Smith Street to reach Royal Hospital Road. Charles II founded this home in 1682 for elderly army veterans to be lodged, nourished and nursed whenever they fall ill. Today some 350 veteran soldiers are looked after here. The smart ceremonial dress of the Chelsea Pensioners is a bright scarlet uniform and three-cornered hat. The hospital itself is a fine building by Christopher Wren, complete with museum and chapel. Every May, the renowned Chelsea Flower Show is held in the delightful grounds. • Mon–Sat 10am–noon and 2–4pm, Sun from 2pm ☎ 7881 5200 (call in advance as changes are frequent) • Royal Hospital Road, SW3 ⊖ Sloane Square/South Kensington

Chelsea Physic Garden (map 4, B8) On the way towards the embankment, this lovely garden of fragrant, colourful blooms was founded in 1673 and originally conceived as a means of investigating the medicinal properties of plants. The story it tells about the history of plants and crops and their influence on modern life is fascinating. • Apr–Oct, Wed noon–5pm, Sun 2–6pm; during Chelsea Flower Show open daily noon–5pm • 66 Royal Hospital Road, SW3 ⊖ Sloane Square/South Kensington

Battersea Park (map 4, B8) From the Chelsea Embankment, cross the river by Albert Bridge to this attractive park, created in the Victorian era to improve the living conditions of the crowded poor districts. There's an ornamental lake, a butterfly reserve, deer park, zoo, flower gardens and sports facilities. The Peace Pagoda was donated by the Japanese as a memorial to Hiroshima in 1945. • Daily 8am–dusk • Albert Bridge Road, SW11; Bus No. 137 from Hyde Park Corner; train from Victoria to Battersea Park

WALKING TOUR: WESTMINSTER

The upmarket district of Knightsbridge is known throughout the world as the home of **Harrods**, an extravagantly luxurious department store on Brompton Road. Be sure to drop in if only to admire the sumptuous Art Deco Food Hall. Fans of modernist architecture might want to make a detour from here along Hans Crescent, next to Harrods, to Sloane Street and the **Danish Embassy** at no. 55, the only London work of renowned Danish architect and designer Arne Jacobsen.

Generally, though, it's Victorian architecture that dominates this part of the capital. A few hundred metres west on the right-hand side of Brompton Road is the Italianate baroque **London Oratory**, dating from 1884. Just west of the church on Cromwell Road is the start of the area known informally as "Albertopolis". Evidence of the fruition of Albert's vision is immediately visible on leaving the Oratory in the striking façade of the **Victoria and Albert Museum**. Turn right onto Exhibition Road; on the opposite side are the two other major museums of Albertopolis, the **Natural History Museum** and the **Science Museum**.

Keep going along Exhibition Road and turn left onto **Imperial College** Road. Imperial College is a leading science-based college within London University formed from the science schools that flourished here in the 19th century. The **Imperial Institute Tower** 85 m (279-ft) high, is all that remains of the institute founded after the Imperial Exhibition of 1886. Return to Exhibition Road and head left as far as Prince Consort Road. On the left is the **Royal College of Music**, which counts Vaughan Williams and Benjamin Britten among its alumni and also puts on regular concerts. Take the time to study **Albert Court** on the other side of Prince Consort Road, a remarkable turreted seven-storey apartment block dating from 1890.

Behind Albert Court is one of the crowning glories of Albertopolis, the **Royal Albert Hall**. A huge elliptical concert hall holding up to 8000 people, it's now the home of the summer Proms festival. Across from the hall just inside Kensington Gardens is the **Albert Memorial**, a splendid High Victorian monument to Albert that has a sculpture of the prince sitting inside an ornate neo-Gothic shrine.

From here, return along Exhibition Road to South Kensington station.

WESTMINSTER 55

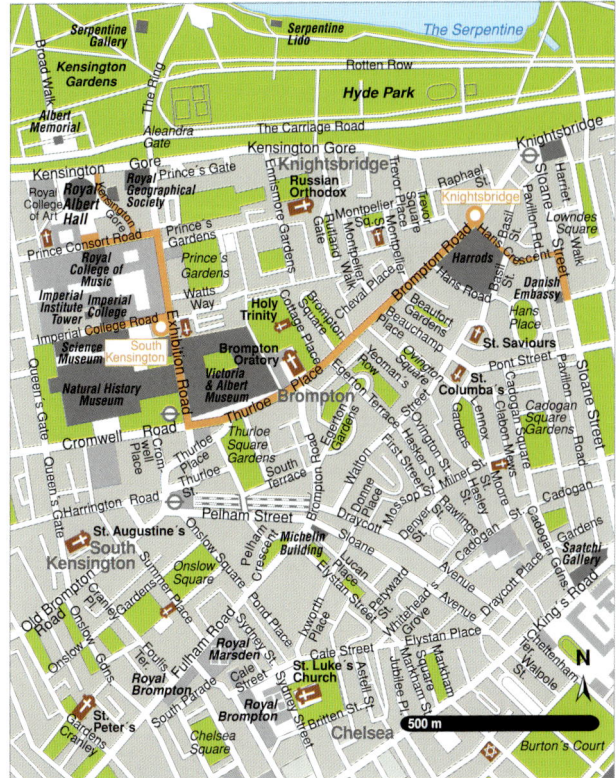

VICTORIAN VISION

The Great Exhibition of 1851 made a substantial profit and Prince Albert, Queen Victoria's consort, suggested that it be used to build a "cultural quarter".

Start: ⊖ Knightsbridge **Finish:** ⊖ South Kensington

MARKET ECONOMIES

London has a handful of markets that have become famous throughout the country and far beyond, and which are now as much essential cultural experiences for visitors as going to the V&A or the National Gallery. The colourful cries and calls of the stallholders and the crowds that consist of people from all corners of the globe transform them into living theatre, though it's a theatre where the audience might come away with an old leather jacket, an antique silver brooch or a second-hand CD. Some markets attract a resolutely trendy clientele; others appeal more to the bargain hunter out to make a killing. But they all provide a marvellous spectacle and cost nothing to look around—a genuine free market in action, one might say.

Cool marketing

Camden Market is centred on Camden High Street, northwest of Regent's Park. It's a good place to go for low-price designer clothes, jewellery and handicraft items, as well as to check out the cool young things of NW1. Shops and most stalls open daily.

The **Portobello Road Market** in Notting Hill was always a magnet for smart, affluent locals searching for just the right antique vase, candelabra or decorative ornament to set off their elegant west London homes; and for a more alternative crowd, who come for the chic party clothes and organic food stalls. Since the Hugh Grant film *Notting Hill*, of course, it has also become a magnet for tourists. Saturdays, 8am–6pm.

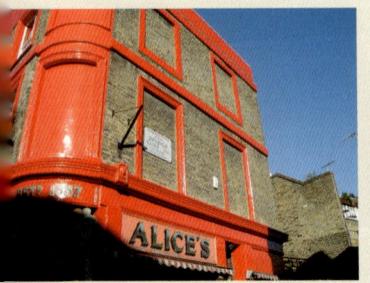

Spitalfields, on Commercial Street, E1, is currently one of London's trendiest areas, and its historic market is the kind of place where East End barrow boys mingle with millionaire city slickers. On sale here are arts and crafts items, second-hand books, organic foodstuffs, and clothes with lashings of street-cred. Every day except Saturday.

Anything goes
Petticoat Lane Market has its origins in the 18th century when Huguenot weavers and Jewish tailors and traders had moved into this part of the East End; today it's predominantly a second-hand clothes market, though the cockney stallholders are as much fun as the bargains on offer. Open all day Monday to Friday, and on Sundays to 2pm.

Nearby **Brick Lane Market** is a raucous bric-a-brac extravaganza spreading into several side streets, where you might find anything from a bargain antique lamp or a computer to old magazines or comics, shoe laces, tiger rugs and cheap shampoo. Sundays 9am–2pm.

In London's lively markets you'll find everything collectible from African Art to Victoriana.

SOUTH BANK

For centuries, London's south bank was a sordid periphery of brothels, bear-baiting pits and various other forms of lowlife to which the good folk of the City would go for illicit entertainment. It was also where the main theatres were built to avoid London's strict licensing laws, and many of Shakespeare's greatest plays were first performed here at the Globe. By the 19th century, the south bank had become an important area of London's urban expansion, with warehouses, wharves and a vast sprawl of residential districts. But the new millennium has seen it come into its own; an array of daring architectural projects have come to fruition, and there are fine museums and arts complexes, as well as the Thames Path, a riverside walkway that offers a traffic-free view of the city's skyline.

THE DISTRICT AT A GLANCE

SIGHTS

Architecture
Southwark Cathedral 60
Millennium Bridge ...62

Art
Tate Modern ★ 62
Dali Universe 62

Underwater
London Aquarium 62

Views
BA London Eye ★ 62

Museums
Brunel Engine House and Tunnel Exhibition 58
Design Museum........59
HMS Belfast ★ 59
Winston Churchill's Britain at War Experience...............60
London Dungeon 60

Bramah Tea & Coffee Museum 60
Shakespeare's Globe Theatre and Exhibition ★ 61
Florence Nightingale Museum..................63
Imperial War Museum ★ 63

WALKING TOUR 64

WINING AND DINING 92

Brunel Engine House & Tunnel Exhibition (map 3, I3) The exhibition is located in the engine house of what was the first underwater tunnel in the world, completed in 1843 and masterminded by Marc Brunel, father of the

The Design Museum—a great place to stimulate the imagination.

more famous Isambard Kingdom. The tunnel itself is now used by the trains of the East London line. • **Daily 10am–5pm** • **Railway Avenue, Southwark, SE1** ⊖ **Rotherhithe**

Design Museum (H5) This converted 1950s docklands warehouse exhibits the best in industrial design and graphics from the 1950s to the present. There's a good bookshop and restaurant. • **Daily 10am–5.45pm (last admission 5.15pm)** • **Shad Thames, SE1** ⊖ **London Bridge/Tower Hill**

HMS Belfast (H4) Now calmly moored on the Thames, this huge warship played an important role in the D-Day landings of World War II and also saw active service in the Korean War in the 1950s. Climb aboard and explore the cabins, engine rooms and gun turrets of its seven decks. • **Daily Mar–Oct 10am–6pm (last admission 5.15pm); Nov–Feb 10am–5pm (last admission 4.15pm)** • **Morgan's Lane, Tooley Street, SE1** ⊖ **London Bridge**

Winston Churchill's Britain at War Experience (H5) Walk inland and you'll soon arrive at Tooley Street. The museum explores the effects of World War II on the lives of ordinary people, illustrating how they coped with rationing, blackouts and air-raids. There's a frightening re-creation of the Blitz. • Daily Apr–Sept 10am–5.30pm, Oct–Mar 10am–4.30pm • 64–66 Tooley Street, SE1 ⊖ London Bridge

London Dungeon (H5) A little further along Tooley Street, this is a horror museum that's certainly not for the very young or very sensitive. Its state-of-the-art effects and waxworks will give you the creeps—there's plenty of torture and death, a Jack the Ripper show and a very realistic Great Fire. • Daily 10am–5pm • Tooley Street, SE1 ⊖ London Bridge

Southwark Cathedral (G5) Just beyond London Bridge, Southwark Cathedral is the fourth church to be erected on the site. Rebuilt in Gothic style in the 13th century, it enjoyed its heyday as an Augustinian priory church in the diocese of the Bishops of Winchester. As the point of entry for London, Southwark was an important market town; the church gave sanctuary to its debtors, criminals and prostitutes. After the Reformation, it became run-down, and parts of it were used as a bakery and pigsty. In the 19th century the cathedral was restored to its former glory. In 1424, James I, King of Scotland, was married here to the niece of Cardinal Beaufort, Bishop of Winchester. Look for the cardinal's hat and coat-of-arms engraved on a pillar in the south transept. In Elizabethan times, the cathedral was the parish church of Shakespeare, who worked at the nearby Globe Theatre—his brother Edmund is buried here. There are some interesting plaques, such as the monument to John Harvard, founder of Harvard University, who was baptised in the cathedral. • Daily 8am–6pm; organ recitals Mon 1.10pm, concerts Tues 1.10pm • Borough High Street, SE1 ⊖ London Bridge

Bramah Tea & Coffee Museum (G5) This museum is dedicated to London's longstanding trade in tea and coffee. The story is told through historical prints, pictures and maps, complemented by a remarkable collection of tea and coffee-making equipment, including some remarkable teapots, among them the world's largest. Real tea, as opposed to the tea-bag kind, is served in the café.

• Open daily 10am–6pm • 40 Southwark Street, SE1 ⊖ London Bridge (exit Borough High Street)

Shakespeare's Globe Theatre and Exhibition (G4) Back on the riverside past Southwark Bridge, a replica of Shakespeare's old Globe Theatre, complete with thatched roof, has risen a short distance from the excavated site of the original, thanks to the perseverance of American actor Sam Wanamaker. Guided tours show you the materials, techniques and craftsmanship that went into its re-creation. Plays are staged in the summer months, in conditions similar to those experienced by both actors and audience in Shakespeare's day (at which times visits are restricted). • **Daily May–Sept 9am–noon; Oct–Apr**

THE POWER OF ART

When Bankside Power Station opened in 1963 it met with criticism from those who thought it was in too prominent a spot for such a massive modern building. But its architect, Sir Giles Gilbert Scott (1880–1960), had already designed Battersea Power Station and Waterloo Bridge, as well as the classic red telephone box, and proved himself a master at fusing historical forms with modern industrial structures. Bankside is best seen, perhaps, as a cathedral of the industrial age, with a great central spire—the chimney—and, in the turbine hall, a dramatic, cavernous inner space. In 1990, Bankside became the inspired choice for a dedicated museum of modern art from the Tate Gallery's vast collection. The main galleries are located in the former boiler house, while a string of contemporary artists have risen to the exciting challenge of the turbine hall.

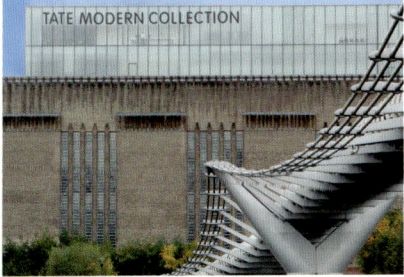

10am–5pm ☏ 7902 1500 for information on plays • New Globe Walk, Bankside, SE1 ⊖ Blackfriars/London Bridge

Tate Modern (F4) In a former power station, the gallery displays modern art from 1900 onwards and introduces new art as it is created. Laid out by theme, the rooms juxtapose classic 20th-century versions of the great tradition—a Monet lily pond, Picasso's *Weeping Woman*—with works by contemporary artists. Shops and 7th-floor café with view of St Paul's. • Sun– Thurs 10am–6pm, Fri–Sat 10am–10pm • Bankside, SE1 ⊖ Blackfriars/ Southwark

Millennium Bridge (F4) In front of the Tate Modern, the slim, elegant bridge in stainless steel and aluminium was designed by sculptor Anthony Caro and architect Norman Foster, and opened by the Queen in May 2000. A pedestrians-only crossing and the first new bridge location across the Thames since the Victorian era, it was conceived as a "blade of light" over the Thames. Energy-dissipating dampers were fitted retroactively when the bridge was found to sway alarmingly. It was re-opened in 2002. ⊖ Blackfriars/Southwark

BA London Eye (E5) Past the South Bank arts complex is the world's largest observation wheel. Journey time is about 30 minutes and each of the 32 capsules can take 25 people. The view from 135 m (443 ft) above the Thames is breathtaking. • Ticket office open daily from 9.30am; flights June–Sept 10am–9pm; Oct–May 10am–8pm; times subject to change: see www.ba-londoneye.com for details ☏ 870 990 8883/groups 0870 5000 600 • Millennium Pier, South Bank, SE1 ⊖ Waterloo/Westminster/Embankment

Dali Universe (E5) Spindly-legged elephants and giant snails, the famous red sofa in the shape of Mae West's lips, and a canvas created for Hitchcock's film Spellbound are just a few of the 500 works by Dalí on display. • Daily 10am–5.30pm; late-night openings in summer • County Hall, Riverside Building, Westminster Bridge Road, SE1 ⊖ Waterloo/Westminster

London Aquarium (E5) This is one of Europe's largest exhibits of fish and other sea creatures. • Daily 10am–6pm, last admission 5pm • County Hall, Riverside Building, Westminster Bridge Road, SE1 ⊖ Waterloo/Westminster/

Traditional timber construction methods were used to resurrect Shakespeare's Globe Theatre; the original burnt down in 1613.

Florence Nightingale Museum (E5) Florence Nightingale, named after her place of birth, established the world's first School of Nursing at St Thomas's Hospital in 1860. This museum looks at her many achievements during a long life of public service, though she's still best known for her moment in the media spotlight during the Crimean War when she acquired her nickname, the Lady with the Lamp. • Daily 10am– 4.30pm, last admission 4pm ☎ 7620 0374 • Lambeth Palace Road, SE1 ⊖ Westminster, and walk over Westminster Bridge

Imperial War Museum (F6) Housed in the former Royal Bethlehem Hospital, the museum opened in 1920 in the aftermath of World War I as part of the attempt to make sense of that catastrophe. Subsequent conflicts are looked at with equal sensitivity: life in the trenches, the Blitz, the Holocaust. • Daily 10am–6pm; free admission • Lambeth Road, SE1 ⊖ Lambeth North/ Elephant & Castle

WALKING TOUR: SOUTH BANK

Turn left from Rotherhithe station onto Railway Avenue, site of the **Brunel Engine House & Tunnel Exhibition**. Continue along the avenue to the river, stopping at St Marychurch Street to see **St Mary's**. The current building dates from 1715, but the previous one was the parish church of the *Mayflower*'s crew. Christopher Jones, the ship's captain, is buried in the churchyard.

Head along **Thames Path** towards Tower Bridge. This area of wharves and warehouses is now a place of desirable waterfront apartments and trendy bars and cafés. Overlooking the river at Shad Thames on the other side of St Saviour's Dock is the **Design Museum**.

Carry on along the riverbank past Tower Bridge. The round glass structure on your left is **City Hall**, designed by leading contemporary British architect Norman Foster. Walk past the massive bulk of *HMS Belfast* docked on the river and beyond London Bridge to the atmospheric, narrow streets around Southwark Cathedral. For centuries this was where Londoners came to gamble, watch the latest Shakespearian drama or visit brothels. The area was owned by the Bishops of Winchester, whose wealth was boosted by fines imposed on prostitutes (known colloquially as "Winchester Geese"). If you continue to the right from the cathedral you'll arrive at Clink Street, where the only surviving remnant of medieval Winchester Palace is a large rose window that once decorated its great hall. In a cellar a few steps from here is **Clink Prison Museum**. This was also run by the Bishops of Winchester, and its notorious brutality made "going to the Clink" a byword for being sent to prison that's still in use in England today.

Clink Street leads to Southwark Bridge. On the other side is **The Anchor**, a superb 18th-century inn with a fine viewing platform on the Thames where you can enjoy a pint and a great view of St Paul's. The modern reconstruction of Shakespeare's **Globe Theatre** is a little further along Bankside, and just beyond this is a row of small 18th-century houses. No. 49 has a plaque claiming this is where Christopher Wren stayed during the construction of St Paul's. Continue to the enormous brickwork structure of the Bankside power station—now **Tate Modern**. From here you can cross the river via the Millennium Bridge and carry on up to St Paul's.

SOUTH BANK

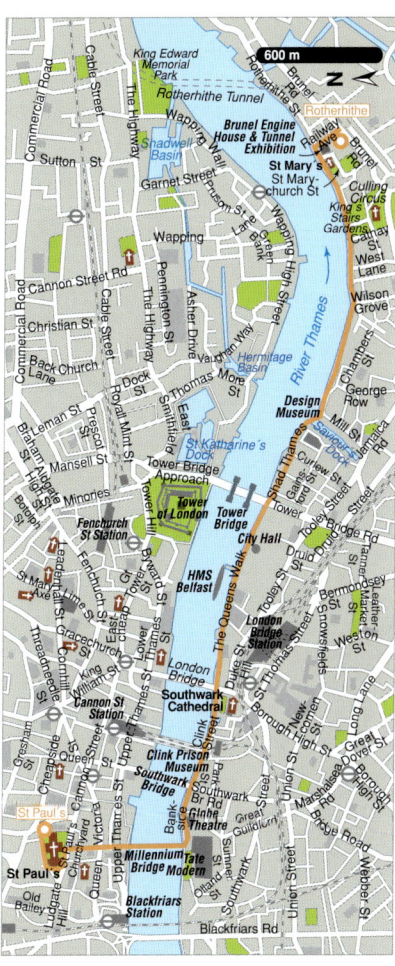

ALONG THE WATERFRONT

History in architecture, from Shakespeare's Globe to the Millennium Bridge.

Start:
⊖ Rotherhithe

Finish:
⊖ St Paul's

WHAT'S IN A NAME?

There are many alternative terms used by Londoners to describe the everyday things found in the city they live in, and many nicknames—often uncomplimentary—for the new buildings that have sprung up over the past few decades. Visitors to the city might well find it useful to be aware of some of these, if only to understand what the natives are actually talking about.

Common expressions

As the possessor of the world's first underground train system, London secured the patent on the most literal and descriptive name for it: the Underground. This is too simple, of course, so Londoners complicate matters by referring to it almost universally as "the Tube".

Following in this vein, the tiny City of London—as opposed to the vast city called London—is also known as the Square Mile, a reference to the original boundaries set by the Roman founders a couple of thousand years ago. You can't accuse Londoners of not respecting tradition, at least: policemen are still called Bobbies even though it's a reference to Sir Robert Peel, who as Home Secretary created the first Metropolitan police force in London in 1829. You'll also hear them referred to as "Coppers",

Left: Norman Foster's "Gherkin" has won many prestigious prizes.
Right: its wobble has been stabilized, but the name has stayed.

which derives from "to cop", an old English word meaning to catch, and as "The Bill" or "Old Bill", which has a variety of possible etymologies including Robert Peel's original Metropolitan Police Bill; King William IV (Old Bill), who came to the throne a year later; or old constables of the watch, who were sometimes named for the bills, or billhooks, they carried as weapons.

On the other hand, should someone suggest a trip to the "boozer" you won't need to call the Old Bill as it means nothing more sinister than going to the pub.

Modern nicknames

The prevalence of unflattering nicknames for new additions to London's cityscape reflects the typical Londoner's delight in cutting pretentiousness down to size. Buckingham Palace might be the most famous palace in the world, but to locals it's known as the less grandiose Buck House. Modern architecture has come in for far rougher treatment. The Princess Diana Memorial Fountain in Hyde Park earned the immediate nickname of the "Storm Drain", while the Millennium Bridge in front of Tate Modern is still called "Wobbly Bridge" because of the initial period when it had to be closed due to excessive swaying. But it's the nickname given to Norman Foster's brand new Swiss Re tower at 30 St Mary Axe that has gained the most widespread acceptance, and it now used throughout the City. In fact, ask anyone for the Swiss Re tower and they'll probably look blank; ask for the "Gherkin" and they'll point you in the right direction. And when you see it, you'll know why.

EAST END AND DOCKLANDS

The East End has long been an area inhabited by London's poorest communities. This started in the 16th century when metalworkers were forced to move there. Its cheap housing made it the natural destination for waves of immigrants, from 17th-century Huguenots to the Bengalis of the 1960s and 70s. An image developed of the East End as a place of lawlessness—it's also where Jack the Ripper terrorized the population in Victorian times. Today, much of it has been gentrified.

THE DISTRICT AT A GLANCE

SIGHTS

Architecture
Christ Church, Spitalfields ★ 70
Docklands 70
Historic Maritime Greenwich ★ 71
Thames Barrier ★ 71

Art
Whitechapel Art Gallery 70

Browsing
Petticoat Lane ★ 69
Brick Lane Market 70

Museums
Dennis Severs' House 68
Geffrye Museum 69

Bethnal Green Museum of Childhood 70

WALKING TOUR 72

WINING AND DINING 92

Dennis Severs' House (H2) A restored Georgian house, seemingly trapped in the early 18th century, when it was inhabited by a Huguenot family of weavers. As you wander around you feel as if the family were still at home ; the smell of their dinner lingers, the stairs creak, a clock chimes, horses pass by, clip-clopping on the cobblestones. The American artist Dennis Severs resided here until his death in 1999 and kept the house without heat, electricity or running water ; he bequeathed it to the Spitalfields Historical Housing Association. • Open 1st and 3rd Sun of month, 2–5pm; Mon after 1st and 3rd Sun noon–2pm; candlelit Silent Night every Mon except Bank Holidays, times vary according to sunset. Book in advance ☎ 020 7247 4013 (9.30am–3pm), fax 020 7377 5548 • 18 Folgate St, Spitalfields E1 ⊖Liverpool St

EAST END AND DOCKLANDS

The Docklands has become a desirable area to live in.

Geffrye Museum (H1) Located in a group of former ironmongers' almshouses dating from 1715, this is one of London's hidden gems. It was converted into a museum of furniture and interior design early in the 20th century and provides a fascinating journey through history via the domestic setting of the living room. Starting with the Elizabethans, and moving on to the Georgians and Victorians, you finally arrive at the modern era, with a high-tech 1990s' interior appropriately placed in the museum's jazzy new extension. • Tues–Sat 10am–5pm, Sundays and bank holidays noon–5pm; restaurant open until 4.45pm; walled herb garden and period garden rooms April to October during museum opening hours. ☎ 7739 9893 • 136, Kingsland Road, E2 ⊖ Liverpool Street, then bus 242 or 149 from Bishopsgate; or Old Street (exit 2) then bus 243 or 15 minutes' walk

Petticoat Lane (H3) London's legendary Sunday morning market began specializing in the cloth trade after Huguenot weavers and Jewish traders settled in the district. It now sells a bit of everything, and boasts some of the most colourful and persuasive pedlars in the capital. It's one of the best shows in town, but be prepared to haggle. • **Middlesex Street, E1** ⊖ **Liverpool Street/Aldgate/ Aldgate East**

Whitechapel Art Gallery (H3) Follow Whitechapel High St from the bottom of Middlesex Street to this fine building dating from 1899. The gallery puts on some of London's most exciting exhibitions of art by contemporary British and international artists. • **Tues–Sun 11am–6pm, Thurs till 9pm** ☎ **7522 7888/ 7878** • **80–82 Whitechapel High St, E1** ⊖ **Aldgate East**

Christ Church, Spitalfields (H3) Head north up Commercial Street to this superb Nicholas Hawksmoor church, built in 1714 for use by the Huguenot community. Its huge portico has four Tuscan columns, and the unusual English baroque tower is topped by a spire 69 m (226 ft) high. Nearby, the eye-catching Spitalfields market hall is worth checking out, with stalls selling books, clothes, organic food and arts and crafts. • **Commercial Street, E1** ⊖ **Aldgate East/ Liverpool Street**

Brick Lane Market (H2) Walk along Fournier Street just north of Christ Church to arrive at this street revered for its curry houses, clothes and food shops. Its Sunday market is a bastion of South Asian culture in the heart of the East End, its stalls stacked with spices, rugs and fabrics. • **Sun 5am–2pm** • **Brick Lane, E1** ⊖ **Aldgate East/Shoreditch**

Bethnal Green Museum of Childhood (map 3, I1) The national museum of childhood is bound to fascinate children and their parents, too. There are fabulous collections of toys, children's costumes and nursery antiques, and 50 delightful doll's houses. • **Mon–Sun 10am–5.50pm** • **Cambridge Heath Road, E2** ⊖ **Bethnal Green**

Docklands (map 3, I3–J4) London's once great dockyard area rose to vast scale and importance during Britain's imperial heyday in the 19th century and collapsed rapidly into disuse after the advent of deep-water container ships in the 1960s. In the 1980s, the government decided to make the area a show-

piece of urban renewal. Its centrepiece is the striking, massive steel block of Cesar Pelli's One Canada Square building, the tallest in Britain at 246 m (807 ft). Stay on board the DLR train till Island Gardens for a marvellous view of Christopher's Wren's Royal Hospital across the river at Greenwich—after which you can use the Greenwich Foot Tunnel, built in 1902, to get there.
⊖ or DLR Canary Wharf; DLR Island Gardens

Historic Maritime Greenwich (map 3, K4) This historic complex is light and airy, dotted with parks, museums and, at weekends, markets. Start with Wren's breathtaking Royal Hospital. William and Mary established it for retired seamen, and in 1873, the institution was turned into the Royal Naval College. Visitors have access to the Painted Hall—the refectory—and the chapel. The National Maritime Museum occupies several buildings, the central part being the exquisitely restored Queen's House, built by Inigo Jones in the 17th century for Charles I's wife Henrietta Maria. Look for the Tulip Staircase and the painted bedroom ceiling. The wings hold a huge collection of ships, nautical paintings and memorabilia and navigational instruments. The Old Royal Observatory of Christopher Wren has undergone a long refurbishment, with many new features, including a sound show in the Telescope Dome and a new presentation of the Greenwich Mean Time Meridian. If you're there at 1pm, you will see the red time ball drop on Flamsteed House's eastern turret so that ships passing can check their chronometers. The seagoing vessels *Cutty Sark*—a tea clipper from 1869—and *Gipsy Moth IV* are moored at the river. • **Museums daily 10am–5pm** ☎ 8858 4422 • Greenwich, SE10; DLR: Cutty Sark

Thames Barrier (map 3, M3) A couple of miles downstream, huge, shiny steel fins distinguish the ten gates of the world's largest movable flood barrier. The Thames tides, which in the past would rise as much as 7 m (24 ft) in spring, are now under control. The Visitors' Centre gives background information on the construction and operation, using video displays, a working model and an audio-visual show. • **Visitors' Centre: April–Sept Mon–Sun 10.30am–4.30pm, rest of the year 11am–3.30pm; last show one hour before closing time** ☎ 8305 4188 • Unity Way, Woolwich, SE18 • Train from Charing Cross to Charlton Station (bus or 20-minute walk, see information) or ⊖ to North Greenwich

WALKING TOUR: EAST END

On leaving the south exit of Liverpool Street Station, pause for a look at the restored Victorian magnificence of the **Great Eastern Hotel**, which opened in 1884 and once had seawater brought in by train so that its guests could enjoy restorative seawater baths. Continue east along Liverpool Street and turn left onto **Bishopsgate**, an ancient Roman route leading north out of London. This crosses Middlesex Street on the right, which on Sunday mornings is home to the colourful Petticoat Lane market, though a smaller market is also held from Monday to Friday.

Take the second turning on the right after this along **Brushfield Street**. This passes the historic **Spitalfields Market** with its superb vaulted roof, and leads to Commercial Street. Diagonally to the right is Nicholas Hawksmoor's stunning **Christ Church Spitalfields**, designed in 1714 for the Protestant Huguenot refugees who had recently moved into East London to escape religious persecution in France: in fact, more than half the names on the gravestones here are French. Spitalfields also has a darker history. At 84 Commercial Street is the **Ten Bells** pub, the place where Mary Jane Kelly, one of Jack the Ripper's last victims, was a regular customer. The notorious serial killer haunted the Spitalfields area and killed 11 women in 1888 but was never caught.

Continue east along Fournier Street, opposite Brushfield Street, to **Brick Lane**, at the heart of what has become known as Bangla Town. It's filled with curry houses and sari shops. On the corner of Fournier Street and Brick Lane is the Jamme Masjid, which began as a Huguenot chapel in the 18th century, was converted into a synagogue till the 1960s, and is now a mosque.

Head south along Brick Lane to **Whitechapel Road**. A couple of blocks to the right is the Whitechapel Art Gallery, a cutting edge centre for modern art. At no. 80–82 Whitechapel Road, the **Whitechapel Bell Foundry** has been in business for centuries and is where Liberty Bell in Philadelphia and Big Ben in the Houses of Parliament were forged. Continue east along Whitechapel Road to Whitechapel underground station.

EAST END AND DOCKLANDS

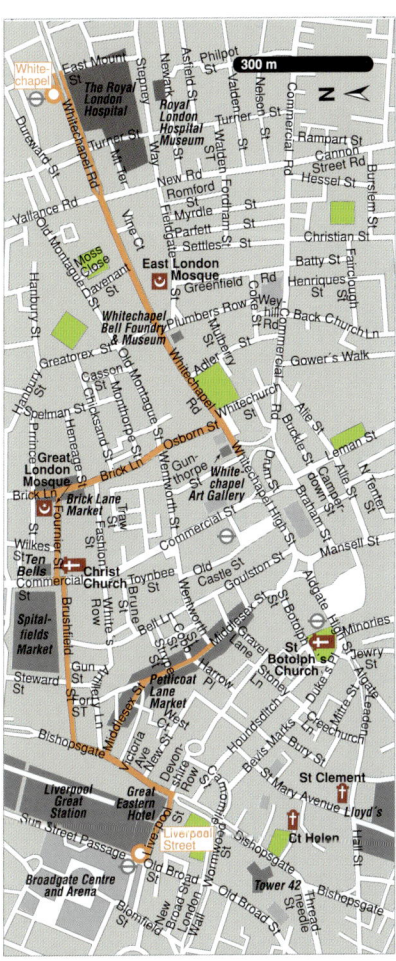

THE EAST END

The East End has seen many different waves of immigration over the centuries; the most recent has been from the Indian sub-continent.

Start:
⊖ Liverpool St

Finish:
⊖ Whitechapel

MINE'S A PINT!

Without doubt, the pub (short for "public house") is at the heart of English social life, which is why the country's two top television soap operas—*Coronation Street* and *Eastenders*—are centred on their respective "local" (the term used for the pub you frequent near to where you live). Over the years, though, London's pubs have undergone many changes. Gone are the days when they were the exclusive preserve of male drinkers, while in most parts of the city the two-class pub—with a saloon bar for more genteel drinkers and a rougher, cheaper public bar for working men—has been consigned to history.

Pubs in the 21st century

Pubs have recently faced even bigger shake-ups. From November 2005 they have been able to stay open late into the night, which means that the classic and all too frustrating landlord's cry of "Time, please!" at 11 o'clock doesn't necessarily signal the end of the evening. What's more, smoking has been banned, as from summer 2007, which might well be a revolution too far for some regulars. Some things never change, though: as ever, drinks are always bought at the bar and there's still no need to tip the barman. Another tradition is that when you're with a group, everyone buys a "round" of drinks for the whole group, each person or couple in turn. Many drinkers like to eat a packet of crisps with their beer.

Recommended pubs

Pubs in London now come in all shapes and sizes, from gay and "gastro" to theatre and traditional.

A relaxed, slightly older gay crowd tends to drink at Soho's best-known gay pub, the **Admiral Duncan** on Old Compton Street; the **Two Brewers** at 114 Clapham High St is famed for its lively drag shows and has remained perennially popular. The "gastro-pub" is an invention of the cookery craze of the 1990s. Check out the upmarket **White Horse** which overlooks Parson's Green in southwest London; the classy menu at the **Coach & Horses** on Ray Street in the City; and the **Seven Stars** in Holborn, frequented by well-paid barristers from the nearby Royal Courts who expect nothing less than a plate of decent grub and a quality pint. A rich mix of beer and cutting edge theatre can be found at the **King's Head**, Islington and the **Gate**, above the **Prince Albert** pub in Notting Hill.

In spite of the recent taste for modernizing old pubs there are still lots of traditional-style ones around. The **Jamaica Wine House**, near the Monument, dates from just after the Great Fire (it started life as a coffee house) and has a fine mahogany-panelled interior; the **Princess Louise** on High Holborn is a 19th-century gin palace, filled with large engraved mirrors and sumptuous decor; the **Nag's Head**, 53 Kinnerton St in Knightsbridge, has a wooden frontage, country-pub atmosphere, good real ale on tap, and a no-mobile phones policy. It's a Free House, which means the landlord is not tied to a brewery and can sell whatever beer he chooses. Cheers!

EXCURSIONS

On a day trip from London, it's possible to reach many historic places by regularly scheduled long-distance buses or by train and explore them on your own. If you prefer to let someone else take the strain, you can always book a commercial guided tour. For information on day trips contact the Britain and London Visitor Centre at 1 Regent Street, SW1Y 4XT, or see the website www.visitbritain.com. Train times and ticket prices can be obtained by dialling 08457 484950.

We begin this section with a few sights in the city outskirts, all of which can be reached by the tube, and follow with some interesting excursions further afield, listed in alphabetical order.

DAYTRIPS AT A GLANCE

SIGHTS

Architecture
Chiswick House 76
Hampton Court Palace★ 79
Hatfield House.........80
Leeds Castle 81
Windsor Castle★ 83
Woburn Abbey.........83

Art
Estorick Collection ...77

Atmosphere
Cambridge★.............78
Canterbury 79
Oxford★...................81
Salisbury and Stonehenge★ 82
Stratford-upon-Avon...........................83

Greenery
Hampstead Heath★ .77
Royal Botanic Gardens (Kew)★ 78
Wetland Centre 78

WALKING TOUR 84

Chiswick House Lord Burlington, a patron of the arts and an architect, built himself this Palladian-style country manor in 1725. The upper floor was richly embellished with cherubs, swags and ceiling paintings by William Kent, who also designed the Italianate garden. • Apr–Sept, Wed–Fri, Sun 10am–6pm; Sat 10am–2pm; Oct, Wed–Fri, Sun 10am–5pm; closed Nov–Mar

The Wetland Centre at Barnes transformed a disused reservoir system into an award-winning wildlife park.

☎ 8995 0508 • Burlington Lane, W4 ⊖ Turnham Green, then bus E3, or train from Waterloo

Estorick Collection Established by American art dealer Eric Estorick and located in a fine Georgian house, the collection is dedicated to modern Italian art. It's especially strong on the Italian Futurists (whose credo was "a roaring motor car is more beautiful than the Winged Victory of Samothrace"), though there are also works by internationally renowned artists like Modigliani and de Chirico, and regular temporary exhibitions on special themes such as aviation posters or pasta. • Wed–Sat 11am–6pm, Sun noon–5pm ☎ 7704 9522 • 39a Canonbury Square N1 ⊖ Highbury & Islington, Bus 271

Hampstead Heath In 324 ha (800 acres), the heath has everything from untamed woods to formal parkland. All this, right on the doorstep of central London. You can fly a kite, swim in a pond, fish, walk or jog, and when you're thirsty, head over to the famous Spaniards Inn. Neoclassical Kenwood House at the northeast corner of the heath is open daily (free entry) to show off its Robert Adam library and small collection of Old Masters. • **Open daily 10am–6pm in summer, to 4pm in winter.** ⊖ Hampstead or Belsize Park

Royal Botanic Gardens (Kew) You'll need at least half a day to see this delightful collection of gardens, conservatories and plant research facilities. Stars are the Princess of Wales Conservatory, containing ten different tropical climates and some carnivorous plants, and the Palm House, a Victorian cast-iron greenhouse sheltering botanical species of the rainforest. On the grounds is Kew Palace, where George III lived in surprising simplicity. The estate had already been landscaped in part by Capability Brown when the king inherited it, and the monarch continued assiduously to oversee its improvement, sending his gardener around the world with Captain Cook to find plant specimens. • **Daily from 9.30am; closing times vary; for details see www.rbgkew.org.uk** ☎ 8332 5655 • Kew, Richmond, Surrey ⊖ Kew Gardens

Wetland Centre Walking around this splendid watery wildlife park, you'll find it hard to believe you're close to central London. It was created by transforming a disused reservoir system into more than 30 different wetland habitats, with 300,000 aquatic plants and 30,000 trees planted. A cinema, discovery centre and state-of-the-art observatory have also been built, from where you can watch the impressive variety of wildfowl attracted to the site, including gorgeous kingfishers. There are six birdwatching hides and a three-storey Peacock Tower offering views over the whole landscape. Children's workshops are organized throughout the year; information on www.wwt.org.uk. • **Daily in winter 9.30am–5pm; in summer 9.30am–6pm; last admission 1 hour before closing** • Wildfowl & Wetlands Trust, Queen Elizabeth's Walk, Barnes, London SW13 9WT ⊖ Hammersmith, then bus 283 (Duck Bus shuttle)

Cambridge One of the two ancient English universities, Cambridge was founded in the 13th century and contains a number of splendid college buildings dating from every period from the Gothic onwards. One thing you won't find is a single campus—like its Oxford rival, the university is an amorphous affair, with its colleges spread out among the shops and houses of the town.

Just walking around the various college quads and gardens will give you an idea of the wealth and glory of the university. The classic beauty spot is known as the Backs, where students lazily punt along the River Cam as it winds through lovely meadows, providing dreamy views of the backs of several of the colleges. Two places which shouldn't be missed are the great chapel of King's College, founded by Henry VI in 1441, and the assemblage of Tudor buildings at Trinity College. The list of alumni of this one college alone is remarkable, and includes Isaac Newton, Lord Byron, Wittgenstein and Pandit Nehru. To experience some cultural delights outside the university, take a look at the Fitzwilliam Museum, with its fine art collection boasting works by artists from Titian to Hockney. • **100 km (60 miles) north of London by M11; train from King's Cross and Liverpool Street**

Canterbury Canterbury has been the centre of Christianity in England since St Augustine converted the Saxon King Ethelbert in 597. The medieval walls and historic town centre are dominated by the magnificent cathedral. The church was begun under Archbishop Lanfranc in 1070, although the fine Bell Harry Tower, 72 m (236 ft) high, was not completed till more than 400 years later. The vast interior is stunning, with acres of stained glass, royal tombs and the shrine of Thomas à Becket, murdered here in 1170 under the orders of King Henry II. It was to this shrine that Chaucer's pilgrims were heading as they related The Canterbury Tales, and a museum dedicated both to the book and to 14th-century life in general can be found in the old church on St Margaret's Street. Other museums that take a look at Canterbury's ancient past are the Roman Museum—the town was one of the first to be established after the Roman conquest of AD 43—and the informative Canterbury Heritage Museum on Stour Street, which will fill you in on such intriguing details as the venerated Becket's less than saintly disposition. • **100 km (60 miles) southeast of London by M2; train from Victoria and Charing Cross, or National Express coach from Victoria**

Hampton Court Palace Cardinal Wolsey, who held the post of Lord Chancellor under Henry VIII, should have known better than to flaunt his wealth. In addition to that indelicacy, he proved unable to arrange a divorce for the king so that he could marry Anne Boleyn. To mark his displeasure, Henry relieved the prelate of Hampton Court—and eventually of all his other possessions, too. Visitors can enjoy the state apartments of Henry VIII, as well as the renovated rooms of William III and Queen Caroline. The vast Tudor kitchens—the finest of their period anywhere in the world—are set out as if a feast was in preparation. Save time to see something of the gardens, especially the famous Maze and the Great Vine planted in 1768. Adjoining Bushy Park is a vast tract of natural parkland, roamed by herds of deer. • **End Mar to end Oct, daily 10am–6pm (last ticket 5pm); winter till 4.30pm (last ticket 3.30pm); Maze same hours, last entry 5.15pm summer, 3.45pm in winter** ☎ **0870 752 7777** • **East Molesey, Surrey** ⊖ **Richmond then bus or boat; train from Waterloo or river boat from April to early October (takes 2½–4 hours by boat)**

Hatfield House This stately home was originally a Tudor palace, used by Henry VIII as a country retreat and the place where Elizabeth I grew up. When Sir Robert Cecil acquired it from Elizabeth's successor, James I, he set about completely altering the building, and what you see today is one of the finest Jacobean houses in England. The beautiful formal gardens were laid out by the

Christchurch College, Oxford

great 17th-century designer, John Tradescant. Today Hatfield House is the residence of Lord and Lady Salisbury. • **Daily from Easter Saturday to end Sept; house noon–4pm; West Gardens, shop 11am–5.30pm; East Gardens open Friday only; guided tours weekdays only.** ☎ 01707 262823 • Hatfield, Herts, 33 km (20 miles) north of London by A1(M), junction 4; train from King's Cross

Leeds Castle The fairytale castle, bristling with towers and battlements, is set on two river islands, about 10 km east of Maidstone. It was built in Norman times on the site of a 9th-century Saxon manor house; Edward I fortified it, and later Henry VIII converted it into a comfortable royal palace. The interior is full of splendid furnishings, superb tapestries and paintings dating from the 14th to 19th centuries; in the grounds, black swans glide on the moat, peacocks stroll over the lawns, and you can watch birds of prey in falconry displays. The gardens are always a mass of colour, with wild flowers growing in the woods, roses, Mediterranean plants, and the charming Culpeper garden, named after the famous herbalist. There are balloon flights, concerts, fireworks displays and many other fascinating activities. • **Open daily 10am–4pm; closed on December 25; last ticket sold 3pm, last admission 3.30pm** ☎ 01 622 765400; group bookings 01 622 76 7865 • Maidstone, Kent, 56 km (35 miles) southeast of London by M20, junction 8; train from London Victoria to Bearsted Station with connecting coach shuttle service; National Express coach from Victoria Coach Station

Oxford The city was founded by the Saxons at the confluence of the Thames and Cherwell rivers. Things began to hot up in the 12th century, when the scholarly Henry I built a palace here and students began coming to the town to study. By the 13th century they were banding together in small, monastic-style teaching halls—the first, University College, dates from 1249, making this the oldest university in Britain. The grandest of the colleges nowadays is Christchurch, which even has the city's magnificent Norman cathedral as its college chapel. Enter it by passing beneath the huge Tom Tower and crossing the expansive main quad. The college also boasts the Christchurch Picture Gallery, with a collection that contains works by Leonardo da Vinci and Michelangelo. Oxford has a total of 41 colleges, so you'll need to be selective in your tour.

Ones that should definitely feature on the itinerary, though, are Magdelen College (pronounced 'mawdlin'), which has a beautiful medieval tower and a deer park at the back; Merton College, with some of its original 13th-century buildings still to be seen on Mob Quad; and Queen's College, a baroque masterpiece built by Nicholas Hawksmoor and Christopher Wren. The focus of the university is Radcliffe Square, with its superb circular 18th-century library designed by James Gibbs. Elsewhere, be sure to search out the Ashmolean Museum, with its fine collection of art, ancient artefacts and other rarities such as Guy Fawkes's lantern and Powhatan's cloak, possibly the oldest item of North American clothing in existence. Also see the quirky Pitt Rivers Museum; many of the archaeological and ethnological objects were donated by early explorers and anthropologists. • **90 km (56 miles) west of London by M40; train from Paddington, Oxford Espress or Oxford Tube coaches from Victoria**

Salisbury and Stonehenge There was an Iron Age fort at Salisbury long before the Romans settled here. Later, the Saxons took over and finally the Normans, who called it Sarum. The ruins of the ancient town—known as "Old Sarum"—can be found 3 km (2 miles) north of modern Salisbury. The "new" city dates from the 13th century, when the clergy upped sticks and built a new church beyond the reach of the Norman castle. Completed within 40 years, Salisbury Cathedral is one of the most coherent expressions of English Gothic architecture—although the 124-metre (407-ft) leaning spire is a 14th-century addition. The city centre meanwhile is a marvellous maze of half- timbered houses and narrow medieval streets. If you're here on a Tuesday or a Saturday, you'll find the lively market going on, an event that goes back to the 16th century. Stonehenge is about 15 km (9 miles) to the north of Salisbury. The origins of this Druid-built 5,000-year-old stone circle are shrouded in mystery—no one really knows how the enormous stones were dragged here all the way from Wales, nor to what purpose they were put after the circle's construction. It's now a World Heritage Site and attracts visitors from all over the globe. No matter how familiar the image has become, Stonehenge will still fill you with awe.
• **Stonehenge Heritage Centre open daily in summer 9am–7pm, restricted hours at other times ☎ 08703 331181 • 145 km (90 miles) southwest of London by M3; train from Waterloo or National Express coach from Victoria**

Stratford-upon-Avon Most visitors come to this attractive market town for its associations with Shakespeare. The great Elizabethan playwright was born in a half-timbered house on Henley Street, now a small museum. Also on the Shakespearean itinerary is Nash's House on Chapel Street, whose grounds contain the remnants of the writer's last home, and Holy Trinity Church, where Shakespeare is buried. Anne Hathaway's Cottage, in which Shakespeare's wife grew up, is a little way out of the city at Shottery. After all this, the only way to finish the day is with a performance of one of the Bard's plays at the Royal Shakespeare Theatre, beautifully situated by the river. • For information and bookings at the Royal Shakespeare Theatre. ☎ 0890 609 1110 • 145 km (90 miles) northwest of London by M40 and A46; direct train from Marylebone, or National Express coach from Victoria

Windsor Castle William the Conqueror began it all with an earth and wood fortress; subsequent monarchs upgraded it in stone, enlarged and embellished it. But it was Queen Victoria who gave the castle its present romantic all-towers-and-turrets look. It is said to be the present Queen's favourite residence. Ten monarchs are buried in St George's Chapel, a masterpiece of 15th-century Perpendicular Gothic, with delicate fan-vaulting. The magnificent State Apartments play second fiddle to the doll's house of Queen Mary, a palace in meticulous miniature. • Nov–Feb daily 9.40am–3pm, Mar–Oct daily 9.40am–4pm ☎ 01753 743 900 • Windsor, Berkshire, 50 km (30 miles) west of London by M4; train from Paddington Station or Green Line coach from Victoria (Eccleston Bridge)

Woburn Abbey The 18th-century home of the Duke of Bedford was built on an earlier Cistercian monastery. Within its grand rooms you'll find a wonderful collection of Tudor portraits, as well as paintings by Velázquez and Rembrandt and a roomful of Canalettos. In the grounds is a huge Safari Park, though entrance is only for those with a car, as the lions, tigers and rhinos are allowed to roam free. • Abbey open daily Apr–Sept 11am–5.30pm (last entry 4pm); grounds and deer park daily Apr–Sept 10am–5pm, Oct–Mar (except 24–26 Dec) 10am–4.30pm ☎ 01525 290666 • Woburn, Bedfordshire, 100 km (60 miles) north of London by M1, junction 12 or 13; train from Euston to Flitwick, then taxi

WALKING TOUR: EXCURSIONS

From Archway station, head northwest up Highgate Hill to **Highgate**, which has retained the atmosphere of an elegant village. At the High Street, turn left onto South Grove and left again at Swain's Lane. Walk down here to **Highgate Cemetery**, which sits on either side of the road. The East Cemetery is open to the public and contains the tombs of George Eliot and Karl Marx, whose request for a simple grave was ignored when the present gigantic bust was put in place in 1954. The overgrown, spooky West Cemetery can only be visited on guided tours. Afterwards, take a look at the adjacent **Waterlow Park**, a beautifully landscaped garden containing the Elizabethan-era Lauderdale House and its attractive café.

Return to South Grove and turn left. A couple of blocks on the right-hand side brings you to **The Grove**, Highgate's smartest street and once the home of such figures as Samuel Taylor Coleridge (no. 3), Yehudi Menuhin (no. 2) and Roger Fry (no. 6). Continue up this street and turn left onto Hampstead Lane, which leads to the glorious open space of **Hampstead Heath**. A walk across its 324 ha is always invigorating. Keep to the northern perimeter of the Heath to reach **Kenwood House**, a delightful 17th-century manor house remodelled by Robert Adam in the following century. This now contains the Iveagh Bequest, with paintings by Rembrandt, Vermeer and Van Dyck. Head south across the Heath to **Parliament Hill**, which offers a spectacular panoramic view of London.

Parliament Hill sits above **Hampstead Village**, which, like Highgate, has jealously guarded its sense of independent village life. Descend from the Heath onto Parliament Hill road, turn right onto South End Road and left onto Keats Grove to reach **Keats House**. This is where the Romantic poet John Keats lived from 1818 to 1820 and wrote *Ode to a Nightingale* under the plum tree in the garden. From here, continue to busy Rosslyn Hill and head right, up to the centre of Hampstead, and left at the crossroads onto Heath Street. Opposite is a small road called **Church Row**, which with its 18th-century houses is acclaimed as the loveliest street in Hampstead. From Church Row go north along **Holly Walk** to enjoy a well-earned drink at the 17th-century Holly Bush pub, once frequented by Dr Johnson and James Boswell and still a bastion of rural cosiness in the big city.

EXCURSIONS 85

FROM HIGHGATE TO HAMPSTEAD

A village atmosphere a stone's throw from the city

Start: ⊖ Archway **Finish:** ⊖ Hampstead

cityBites

London's finest restaurants (Aubergine, Le Gavroche, Chez Nico, and so on) are indeed superlative, but their prices are also sky high, and you need to book a table several weeks ahead. We concentrate here on places where you can eat well without breaking the bank, with a few extravagant exceptions for special treats. Listed, too, are some of the capital's best-loved tea rooms and pubs, which exemplify traditional British attitudes towards the business of food and drink.

Note that many restaurants close on Sunday, except, in general, ethnic eateries. Many of the times given here correspond to "last orders".

Prices are indicated as follows:

1 = reasonable (under £25)

2 = medium (£25–£50)

3 = expensive (over £50)

THE CITY

The Place Below
⊖ St Paul's
St Mary-le-Bow,
Cheapside, EC2
☎ 7329 0789
Mon–Fri 7.30am–3.30pm
[1]
Vegetarian restaurant in the church crypt.

St John
⊖ Farringdon
26 St John Street, EC1
☎ 7251 0848
Bar: Mon–Fri 11am–11pm, Sat 6pm–11pm;
Restaurant Mon–Fri noon–3pm, 6–11pm;
Sat 6–11pm
[1]
Minimalist decor; a rich introduction to the earthier side of traditional English cooking. Lots of offal-based dishes.

Top Floor at Smiths
⊖ Farringdon
67–77 Charterhouse Street, EC1
☎ 7251 7950
Mon–Fri noon–2.45pm, 6–10.45pm, Sat 6.30–10.45pm, Sun 12.30–3.45, 7–10.30pm
[1]
The emphasis is on steak, though fish and vegetarian dishes are available. Ground floor restaurant serves breakfast, salads, snacks.

Ye Olde Cheshire Cheese
⊖ Blackfriars
145 Fleet Street, EC4
☎ 7353 6170
Mon–Fri noon–11pm;
Sat noon–3pm, 5.30–11pm;
Sun noon–3pm
[1]
Famous 17th-century restaurant/ pub. Good traditional English dishes like steak-and-kidney pie.

WEST END

Andrew Edmunds
⊖ Oxford Circus
46 Lexington Street, W1
☎ 7437 5708
Mon–Fri 12.30–3pm, 6–10.45pm,
Sat 1–3pm, 6–10.45pm,
Sun 1–3pm, 6–10.30pm
[1]
Modern European fare in a romantic candle-lit setting. More comfortable upstairs. Imaginative wine list.

Atlantic Bar & Grill
⊖ Piccadilly Circus
20 Glasshouse Street, W1
☎ 7734 4888
Bar: Mon–Fri 5pm–3am, Sat to 10.30pm
Restaurant
Mon–Fri 6pm–11pm;
Sat 6–10.30pm
[2]
Drinking in the bar is the main activity of the style-conscious young regulars, though there's also a restaurant. It's less plebeian than a pub and less raucous than a nightclub.

Bentley's
⊖ Piccadilly Circus
11–15 Swallow St, W1
☎ 7734 4756
Mon–Sat noon–11pm
Sun noon–9.30pm
[2]
If you're fond of fish and seafood, this is the place for you.

Biagio Ristorante Pizzeria
⊖ Piccadilly Circus
30 Rupert Street, W1
☎ 7734 9415
Mon–Sat noon–1.30am,
Sun noon–11.30pm
[1]–[2]
Italian cuisine in a venue just off Shaftesbury Avenue, very convenient for several theatres and excellent value.

Boudin Blanc
⊖ Green Park
5 Trebeck Street, W1
☎ 7499 3292
Daily noon–3pm, 6–11pm
[1]
Cosy, rather noisy bistro-style restaurant serving typical French cuisine such as onion soup, goat's-cheese salad and snails.

Claridge's
🚇Bond Street
Brook Street, W1
☎7629 8860
Tea daily 2.30–5.30pm
1 – 2
It's discreet and classy, and serves a sumptuous high tea. Booking essential. Smart casual.

Criterion
🚇Piccadilly Circus
224 Piccadilly, W1
☎7930 0488
Mon–Sat noon–2.30pm, 5.30–11pm
2
A neo-Byzantine deco for one of London's star chefs Marco Pierre White.

Gaucho Piccadilly
🚇Piccadilly Circus
25 Swallow St, W1
☎7734 4040
Mon–Wed 10am–midnight;
Thurs–Sat 10am–3am;
Sun noon–10.30pm
2
A bustling, popular restaurant on four floors serving hunger-busting steaks and South American wines.

Greenhouse
🚇Green Park
27a Hay's Mews
(off Hill St), W1
☎7499 3331
Mon–Fri noon–2.30pm, 6.30–11pm,
Sat 6.30–11pm
3
Traditional British fare brought up to date.

Ikkyu
🚇Goodge Street
67 Tottenham Court Road, W1
☎7636 9280
Mon–Fri noon–2.30pm, 6–10.30pm;
Sun 6–10.30pm
Last orders 9.45pm
1
A real find—a Japanese restaurant serving delicious food at reasonable prices, in rather humble basement premises.

Museum Tavern
🚇Tottenham Court Road
49 Great Russell St, WC1
☎7242 8987
Mon–Sat 11am–11pm, Sun noon–10.30pm
1
Karl Marx used to tipple in this pub when he wanted to take a break from writing *Das Kapital* in the British Museum reading room across the street. The Victorian-era doors still have their etched glass panels. Real ales, fish and chips.

New World
🚇Leicester Square
1 Gerrard Place, W1

WHAT'S FOR BREAKFAST?

In London hotels, breakfast is one institution that hasn't succumbed to Continental or other foreign influences. Traditionally it begins with half a grapefruit, then cornflakes or perhaps porridge, followed by fried or scrambled eggs and bacon, maybe sausages, fried mushrooms and tomatoes, then toast, butter, jam and marmalade. A really opulent breakfast might even include kippers or kedgeree (a curried mixture of smoked haddock, rice, mushrooms and cream).

☎7734 0677
Mon–Sat
11am– 11.45pm;
Sun 11am–10.45pm
2
Chinatown institution: from 11am to 5.45pm, dim sum, fritters, barbecued ribs, etc. from a trolley; from 6pm, normal service.

Ritz Hotel
⊖Green Park
Piccadilly, W1
☎7493 8181
Seatings 1.30, 2.30 and 5.30pm
Reservations essential
1 – 2
Tea—the whole works—in the Palm Court is a glittering if pricey affair. Jacket and tie for men.

Rules
⊖Covent Garden/Charing Cross
35 Maiden Lane, WC2
☎7836 5314
Mon–Sat noon–11.30pm
Sun noon–10.30pm
2
Founded in 1798, this is London's oldest restaurant. Traditional English food: oysters, sirloin of Scotch beef, saddle of mutton and the perfect steak-and-kidney pie, and yummy treacle pudding for afters. Game from its own estate in the Pennines. Beautiful domed glass ceiling in the dining room and wood panelling.

Sherlock Holmes
⊖Charing Cross
10 Northumberland Street, WC2
☎7930 2644
Daily noon–9.45pm
1
Only minimal detective work is needed to find this pub dedicated to the great sleuth. Holmes memorabilia are on show in the main bar; upstairs is a replica of 221b Baker Street and a dining room.

Thai Pot
⊖Leicester Square
1 Bedfordbury, WC2
☎7379 4580
Mon–Sat noon–3pm, 5.30–11.15pm
1
Good Thai food, excellent value for money and pleasant atmosphere.

AROUND WESTMINSTER

Al Bustan
⊖South Kensington
68 Old Brompton Road, SW7
☎7584 5805
Mon–Sat noon–11pm;
Sun noon–10pm
2
Lebanese cuisine served in generous portions.

Thai Pot

Ark
⊖Notting Hill Gate
122 Palace Gardens Terrace, W8
☎7229 4024
Daily noon–3pm, 6.30–11pm (closed Sun evening and Mon lunch)
2
Modern Italian food, with plenty for vegetarians.

Aubergine
⊖South Kensington
11 Park Walk, SW10
☎7352 3449
Mon–Wed noon–2.15pm, 7–10pm (Thurs, Fri to midnight);
Sat 7pm–1am
3
A chic setting for a memorable gastronomic experience. French cuisine, beautifully presented. Book ahead.

Bibendum Oyster Bar
⊖South Kensington
Michelin House
81 Fulham Road, SW3
☎7589 1480
Mon–Sat noon–10.30pm,
Sun noon–10pm
2

Shellfish heaven in the former Michelin tiled garage.

Blue Elephant
⊖ Fulham Broadway
4 Fulham Broadway, SW6
☎ 7385 6595
Mon–Fri noon–2.30pm,
7pm–00.30am,
Sat 7pm–00.30am,
Sun noon–2.30pm,
7–10.30pm
3

Jungle-like foliage and tropical flowers set the scene for truly spectacular Thai cuisine.

Bombay Brasserie
⊖ Gloucester Road
Courtfield Close,
Courtfield Road, SW7
☎ 7370 4040
Daily noon–3pm,
7.30–11.30pm
2 – 3

The best of Bombay cooking enjoyed in classy surroundings. Popular with the upmarket Kensington crowd.

Chutney Mary
⊖ Fulham Broadway
535 King's Road, SW10
☎ 7351 3113
Mon–Fri 6.30–11pm,
Sat 12.30–3pm,
6–11pm,
Sun 12.30–3pm,
6.30–10.30pm
2

Bibendum

Large, elegant restaurant serving curry, freshly prepared and authentically spiced.

Clarke's
⊖ Notting Hill Gate
124 Kensington Church Street, W8
☎ 7221 9225
Mon–Fri 12.30–2pm;
Tues also 7–10pm;
Sat 11am–2pm, 7–10pm
2

Modern British cuisine with a strong emphasis on the use of organically farmed produce. The dining rooms are pleasantly light and airy

Geale's
⊖ Notting Hill Gate
2 Farmer Street, W8
☎ 7727 7528
(no booking)
Mon–Sat 12.30–3pm,
6–10.30pm,
Sun 6–10pm
1

The best fish and chips in London.

Gordon Ramsay
⊖ Sloane Square/South Kensington
68–69 Royal Hospital Road, SW3
☎ 7352 4441
Mon–Fri noon–2pm,
6.30–11pm
3

Once in a while, treat yourself to the delights of some truly haute cuisine, courtesy of the three-Michelin-star chef.

Ken Lo Memories of China
⊖ Victoria
67–69 Ebury Street, SW1
☎ 7730 7734
Mon–Sat noon–3pm,
Mon–Sun 7–11.15pm
2

Excellent Chinese fare in a modern, light setting.

Kensington Place
⊖ Notting Hill Gate
201–205 Kensington Church Street, W8
☎ 7727 3184
Daily noon–3.30pm,
6.30–11.45pm
Sun to 10.15 pm
2

Modern eclectic menu served up to a smart, if noisy, crowd. The set lunch is always good value for money.

River Café
⊖ Hammersmith (plus longish walk or short taxi ride)
Thames Wharf
Rainville Road, W6

☎ 7386 4200
(booking advised)
Mon–Sat 12.30–2.45pm,
7.30–9.30pm;
Sun 1–3pm
`3`

Out of the way, but well worth the trip for the best pasta in London, and with a riverside setting.

Vama
⊖ Sloane Square/South Kensington
438 King's Road, SW10
☎ 7351 4118
Daily noon–3pm,
6.30–11.30pm,
Sun to 10.30pm
`2`

Fine Indian cuisine in a smart setting.

Wodka
⊖ High Street Kensington
12 St Alban's Grove, W8
☎ 7937 6513
Mon–Fri 12.30–2.30pm,
Mon–Sun 6.30–11.15pm
`2`

Polish cuisine. Wide choice of vodkas.

Zafferano
⊖ Knightsbridge
16 Lowndes Street, SW1
☎ 7235 5800
Daily noon–2.30pm,
7–10.30pm
`2`

Top-class Italian restaurant, a mid-priced gem in posh Belgravia.

SOUTH BANK

Blue Print Café
⊖ Tower Hill
Design Museum
Butlers Wharf, SE1
☎ 7378 7031
Daily noon–3pm,
Mon–Sat 6–11pm
`2`

Contemporary British cuisine and fabulous riverside view. Book well ahead for terrace or window seat.

Butlers Wharf Chop House
⊖ Tower Hill
Shad Thames, SE1
☎ 7403 3403
Daily noon–3pm,
6–11.45pm
Closed Sun evening.
`2`

Traditional English grill restaurant by the riverside.

George Inn
⊖ London Bridge
77 Borough High Street, SE1
☎ 7407 2056
Mon–Sat 11am–9.30pm,
Sun noon–9.30pm
`1`

Historic timber-framed coaching inn with external galleries. Outdoor seating in the courtyard, which occasionally serves in summer for performances of Shakespeare.

Livebait
⊖ Waterloo
43 The Cut, SE1
☎ 7928 7211
Mon–Sat noon–11pm,
Sun 12.30–9pm
`2`

This fish restaurant has shot to gastronomic renown.

Oxo Tower Restaurant
⊖ Waterloo/Blackfriars
Oxo Tower Wharf
Barge House Street, SE1
☎ 7803 3888
Mon–Sat noon–2.30pm,
6–11pm,
Sun noon–3pm,
6.30–10pm
`2`

Fantastic 8th-floor views and good cuisine, described as Asian and modern British. Changing ceiling: white by day, blue at night.

Sarkhel's
⊖ Southfields
199 Replingham Road, SW18
☎ 8870 1483
Tues–Sun noon–2.30pm,
Tues–Thurs,
Sun 6–10.30pm,
Fri and Sat 6–11pm
`1` – `2`

This stylish restaurant, run by the former head chef of the Bombay Brasserie, serves some of the best Indian food in London.

EAST END AND DOCKLANDS

Cafe Spice Namaste
⊖ Tower Hill
16 Prescot Street, E1
☎ 7488 9242
Mon–Fri noon–3pm, 6.15–10.30pm, Sat 6.30–10pm
[1]

Out-of-this-world Indian cuisine in a gaily decorated setting.

Lahore Kebab House
⊖ Whitechapel
2 Umberston Street, E1
☎ 7481 9737
Daily noon–midnight
[1]

Enjoy succulent meat off the skewer or even stewed sheep's feet in this authentic Pakistani restaurant. Limited menu. The lamb and spinach gosht is highly recommended.

The North Pole
⊖ Train to Greenwich
131 Greenwich High Road, SE10
☎ 8853 3020
Bar:
daily noon–midnight, Sun to 11.30pm
Restaurant:
Mon–Sat 6.30–10.30pm; Sun 12.30–10pm
[1] – [2]

The restaurant is on the floor above the pub, and serves top-quality French cuisine.

Prospect of Whitby
⊖ Wapping
57 Wapping Wall, E1
☎ 7481 1095
Mon–Sat 11.30am–11pm;
Sun noon–10.30pm
[1]

One of London's most historic pubs, complete with cobbled courtyard, Elizabethan pewter bar and river views—former regulars include Samuel Pepys and Charles Dickens.

RIVERSIDE DINING AND DRINKING

On a pleasant day, there's nothing nicer than a riverside meal or snack. Here are some places with Thameside seating:

Duke's Head, 8 Lower Richmond Road, SW15; ⊖ Putney Bridge.
Canteen, Chelsea Harbour, SW10; bus No. 11 or 22 from Sloane Square.
Blue Print Café, see p. 92.
Pont de la Tour, Butlers Wharf, SE1; ⊖ Tower Hill.
Butlers Wharf Chop House, see p. 92.
People's Palace, Royal Festival Hall, SE1; ⊖ Waterloo.
Quayside Restaurant, 1 St Katharine's Way, E1; ⊖ Tower Hill.
Doggett's Coat and Badge, 1 Blackfriar's Bridge, SE1; ⊖ Blackfriars.
Old Thameside Inn, Pickfords Wharf, SE1; ⊖ London Bridge.
Anchor Bankside, 34 Park Street, SE1; ⊖ London Bridge.
Founder's Arms, Bankside, SE1; ⊖ London Bridge.
Dickens Inn, St Katharine's Way, E1; ⊖ Tower Hill.
Prospect of Whitby, see above.
The Grapes, Narrow Street, E14; DLR: Westferry.

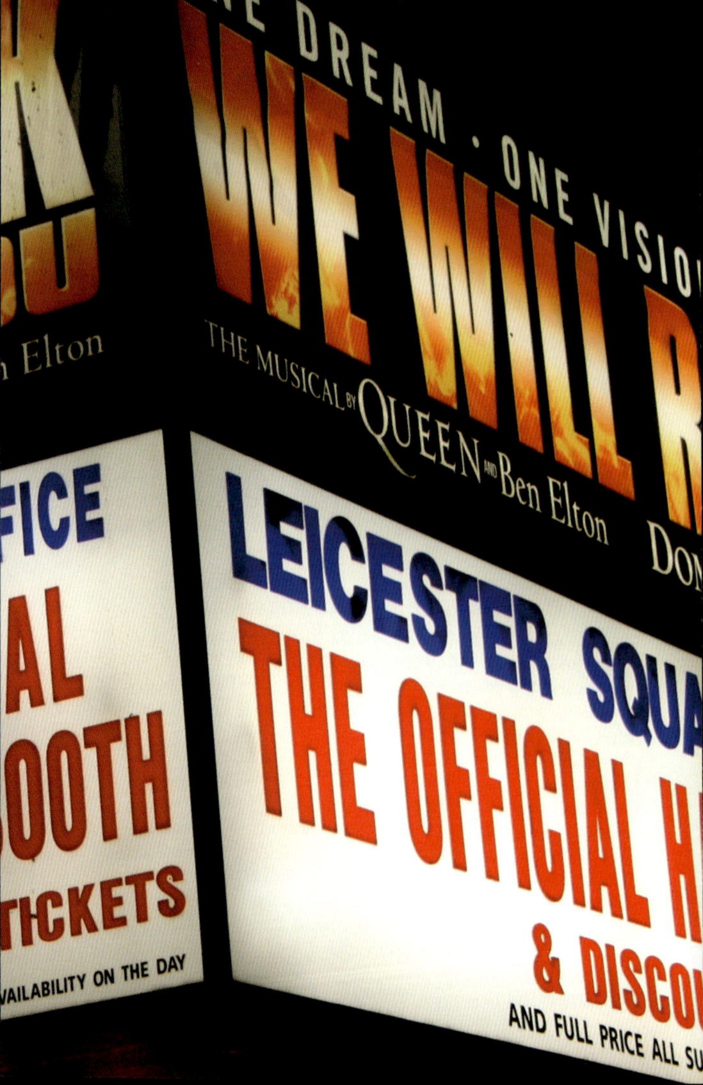

ONE DREAM · ONE VISION

WE WILL R

THE MUSICAL BY QUEEN AND Ben Elton

LEICESTER SQUA

THE OFFICIAL H

& DISCO

AND FULL PRICE ALL S

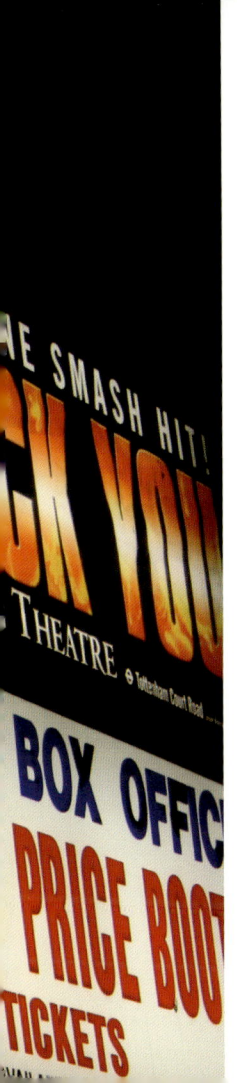

CityNights

In London you'll never be at a loss for something to do on the cultural scene. The city offers the best in opera, dance, theatre, art exhibits, films and concerts. Consult the listings magazines *Time Out* and *What's On* for details or access the Visit London website, www.visitlondon.co.uk.
Getting tickets for shows is never easy. The key is to book as far ahead as possible. Ask your travel agent to help, or phone the box office directly and pay with your credit card. See p. 97 for ticket agencies and information on cut-price tickets.

MAJOR ARTS VENUES

Barbican Arts Centre
⊖ Barbican
Barbican Centre, EC2
☎ 7638 8891 (box office),
7638 4141 (enquiries)
The home of the London Symphony Orchestra, the centre is a veritable maze of concert halls and theatres, linked to several large residential blocks. Yellow markers will help you find your way. Concerts, plays, film, art exhibitions, etc. are all represented. Weekend activities for children.

London Coliseum
⊖ Leicester Square
St Martin's Lane, WC2
☎ 7632 8300
Home of the English National Opera. Considerably less expensive than the Royal Opera House, though productions are usually sung in English, which may deter some.

Royal Academy of Arts
⊖ Piccadilly Circus/Green Park
Burlington House, Piccadilly, W1
☎ 7300 5760
Temporary major art exhibitions are mounted here. The Academy is famous for its annual Summer Exhibition, held from June to August: as many as a thousand artists display their work, which can be purchased by the public.

Royal Albert Hall
⊖ South Kensington
Kensington Gore, SW7
☎ 7589 8212 (box office)
Music of all kinds is performed here, but none is more popular than the Promenade Concerts (known as The Proms), running from July to September and featuring popular classics. The most famous event is the Last Night, when all the "Prommers" join in the resounding finale of a riotous and flag-waving rendering of *Land of Hope and Glory, Rule Britannia* and *Jerusalem*. The entrance price is very low for those prepared to stand.

Royal Opera House
⊖ Covent Garden
Bow Street, WC2
☎ 7304 4000
The Royal Opera and Royal Ballet companies perform their usual and unusual repertoire in these magnificently refurbished headquarters. The new auditorium puts on occasional free lunchtime concerts. There's a public terrace overlooking the Piazza and many shops in the new colonnade. Backstage tours take place at 10.30am, 12.30pm and 2.30pm, except Sundays and matinee days.

Sadler's Wells
⊖ Angel
Rosebery Avenue, EC1
☎ 7863 8000
This acclaimed venue offers internationally renowned and innovative dance, opera and lyric drama.

South Bank Centre
⊖ Waterloo/Embankment
South Bank, SE1
☎ 7452 3000 (Royal National Theatre), 08703 800400 (concert halls)
The biggest arts centre in western Europe consists of the Royal National Theatre comprising the Olivier, Lyttelton and Cottesloe theatres, three concert halls (Royal Festival, Queen Elizabeth and Purcell Room), the National Film Theatre and the Hayward Gallery. The outstanding quality of performances and art at this riverside setting far outshines the massiveness of the premises.

CITYNIGHTS 97

CLUBLAND

Night spots generally offer a regular change of music; dress codes vary. There may be special nights reserved for women or for gays. It's a good idea to phone ahead to check the programme. The private clubs are impossible to get into unless a member friend brings you or you can get help from your hotel receptionist. Following are some of the clubs that admit the public.

Comedy Store
⊖Piccadilly Circus
Haymarket House
Oxendon Street, SW1
☎08700 602 340
Eight or nine comedians will keep you entertained for 2 1/2 hours. Many famous British comedians started out here.

Dingwalls/Jongleurs Comedy Club
⊖Camden Town
Middle Yard
Camden Lock, NW1
☎0870 7870 707 (Jongleurs)
7428 5929 (Comedy)
Mon–Thurs gigs, Fri–Sat shows and dancing, Sun Metal Headz in an old converted warehouse.

Fabric
⊖Farringdom
77a Charterhouse Street, EC11
☎7336 8898
Close to Smithfield's, this club has some of London's meatiest house, electro, techno and hip-hop.

The Fridge
⊖Brixton
Town Hall Parade
Brixton Hill, SW2
☎7326 5100
Large, popular dance spot attracting a multi-ethnic crowd. Trance-techno for a straight crowd on Fridays, major gay scene on Saturdays.

Heaven
⊖Charing Cross/Embankment
Under the Arches
Villiers Street, WC2
☎7930 2020
Mon, Wed 10.30pm–3am,
Sat 10.30pm–5.30am
Sometimes open Fridays
The queen of London's gay and transgender clubbing scene is famous for its high-octane Saturday nights.

Jazz Café
⊖Camden Town
5 Parkway, NW1
☎7534 6955 for box office and enquiries

BOOKING A SEAT

The Visit London office and London Transport information centres can arrange tickets. You can also book them through a reputable agency: Ticketmaster,
☎ 0870 154 4040
www.ticketmaster.co.uk
Keith Prowse Ticketing,
☎ 0870 840 1111
www.keithprowse.com
If you have time and energy to spare, you may want to look for some cut-rate theatre (or opera) tickets.
On the morning of a performance, a limited number of reduced-price day seats are set aside for sale. Students with identification can also get cheap stand-by tickets shortly before curtain time. Come early in both cases and be prepared to queue.
If you don't mind taking pot luck, the Society of West End Theatres (SWET) runs a booth in Leicester Square selling discount tickets for the day's performances. Open at noon for both matinees and evening performances.

Jazz, funk and soul in a converted bank.

Koko
⊖ Camden Town
1a Camden High Street, NW1
☎ 0870 432 5527
The former Camden Palace has been revamped and now mixes opera house décor with one of the coolest rave scenes in the capital.

Ministry of Sound
⊖ Elephant & Castle
103 Gaunt Street, SE1
☎ 08700 600010
Founded in 1991, the Ministry is the superclub of the moment, with a cult following all round the world. It runs its own radio station, produces records and has a custom-built sound system.

Roadhouse
⊖ Covent Garden
The Piazza,
Covent Garden WC2
☎ 7240 6001
Bar, restaurant, live music, DJs. Free entry Mon–Fri before 9pm, Sat before 7.30pm.

Ronnie Scott's
⊖ Leicester Square/ Piccadilly Circus
47 Frith Street, W1
☎ 7439 0747
All the greats have played in the granddaddy of London's jazz clubs.

Stringfellows
⊖ Leicester Square
16–19 Upper St Martins Lane, WC2
☎ 7240 5534
Glamorous place; minor celebrities occasionally to be seen on the glass dance floor. Dress smartly. Table-dancing through the week and disco on Saturday.

Walkabout@Limelight
⊖ Leicester Square
136 Shaftesbury Avenue, WC2
☎ 7255 8630
Intriguing atmosphere in this former Presbyterian chapel reincarnated as an Aussie pub on the ground floor and nightclub in the basement.

OUTDOOR ENTERTAINMENT

Holland Park Open Air Theatre
⊖ High Street Kensington
Holland Park
Kensington High Street, W8
☎ 7602 7856
Opera, drama and dance programmes in a 600-seater outdoor facility, protected from the elements by a canopy. The season runs from June to August.

Kenwood House
⊖ Golders Green/ Archway, then bus 210
Hampstead Lane, NW3
☎ 8233 7435
Bookings through Ticketmaster,
☎ 0870 154 4040
Saturday evenings in summertime, outdoor concerts or opera on the lawn at lakeside, occasionally with a fireworks display. Deckchairs are available, but you may prefer to stretch out on the lawn. Booking essential.

Regent's Park Open Air Theatre
⊖ Baker Street/ Regent's Park
☎ 08700 601 811
Open-air theatre from late May to early September, where the resident New Shakespeare's Company stages classics by the bard himself, Shaw and others. Book several weeks ahead.

LONDON
ON THE BIG SCREEN

For film-makers, London has often been a blank screen onto which they project their own image of the city. In the 1950s, its thick pea-souper fogs and dark alleyways provided a metaphor for tortured psychological states in films such as Jules Dassin's *Night and the City*. Meanwhile, home-grown directors working for the famous Ealing studios found that post-war London's sense of stagnation and quiet desperation provided ripe territory for comedy in movies such as *The Lavender Hill Mob* and *The Ladykillers*. In the decades since then, London has continued to be as important a presence on screen as any of the famous actors who have starred in the films set there.

The Swinging Sixties

An avalanche of movies appeared in the 1960s on the back of London's sudden rise to the status of "the world's coolest city". These range from the eminently forgettable *Here We Go Round the Mulberry Bush* (1967) to the cynical and knowing *Alfie* (1966), which starred Hollywood's favourite cockney actor Michael Caine as a ruthless womanizer. And with pop music as the driving force behind "Swinging London" it's no surprise that The Beatles' first movie, *A Hard Day's Night* (1964), was shot on location around the city, showing the Fab Four cavorting everywhere from Marylebone Station to the Thames towpath at Kew.

However, some of the most interesting films of the period interrogate the image of London as a city of carefree hedonism. Social division and the perennial iniquities of the class system are alive and kicking in *Up the Junction* (1967), set in the working-class district around Clapham Junction in south London. But perhaps the most powerful commentaries on the era come from two off-the-wall art house movies. *Blow-Up* (1966), directed by Italian Michelangelo Antonioni, starts with the photographer-hero, played by an irresistible David Hemmings, being confronted with a possible murder after a photo session in the park (in fact, Maryon Wilson Park in Charlton, southeast London, where the director notoriously painted the paths black and the grass even greener to heighten the effect) and goes on to posit a dark, violent underbelly to a city that sometimes seems to be comprised solely of flowery-shirted beautiful people. In Nic Roeg's *Performance* (1970), starring James Fox and 60s pop icon Mick Jagger, the two lead characters end up in a Notting Hill basement (actually filmed at Powis Square in Bayswater) escaping from the threatening reality of the world outside to something even more disturbing indoors, as the optimism of the swinging sixties descends into drug-induced nightmare.

A kaleidoscope of images

In the years since the 1960s, films based in London have taken several different paths. There is what might be termed the picture-postcard view of London, making the most of its glamorous sights and historic locations. Thus even a tough East End gangster movie like *The Long Good Friday* (1979) didn't shy away from placing its characters in a number of photogenic West End tourist spots, not least of which is the Savoy Hotel in the Strand, from where Bob Hoskins, who plays the gang leader, is abducted in a black cab in the last scene of the film.

A more soft-centred—and hugely popular—movie exploiting London as a location was penned by Richard Curtis: *Notting Hill* (1999) brought together an American box-office star (Julia Roberts) and an English leading man (Hugh Grant) in the unlikely setting of a bookshop on scenic Portobello Road (it's at no 142, although the shop is actually a furniture store). Back in 1965, when Notting Hill was a run-down area of cheap lodgings, it had been the setting of Richard Lester's rather crude comedy *The Knack…and How to Get It*, with a provincial girl played by Rita Tushingham erupting into the world of three frustrated male boarding-house tenants.

Of course, a film like *Notting Hill* almost completely ignores London's complex, multi-cultural status at the start of the 21st century. Stephen Frears' *Dirty Pretty Things* (2002) takes a harder-edged view, however. (He also dealt with the Asian community during the Thatcher years in *My Beautiful Laundrette*, with Daniel Day-Lewis, originally shot for television in 1985 and tackling many issues such as homosexuality and racism.) The gritty urban realist style of *Dirty Pretty Things* sees the capital through the eyes of illegal immigrants from around the world, the ones who keep the city running by driving its minicabs and working as cleaners and night porters in its many hotels. The hotel lobby that features throughout the movie is actually the entrance to Wandsworth Town Hall in southwest London.

Unfortunately, 21st-century urban paranoia is also a feature of life in the big city, something that is encapsulated by Danny Boyle's *28 Days Later* (2002), in which a deadly virus has left the capital eerily quiet. Scenes showing a double-decker bus lying on its side in an empty Whitehall and broken souvenirs strewn across a desolate Westminster Bridge epitomize this apocalyptic vision of the city—though it's fair to say that this will probably be the only time you'll ever see these locations at the heart of London without hordes of people blocking the view…

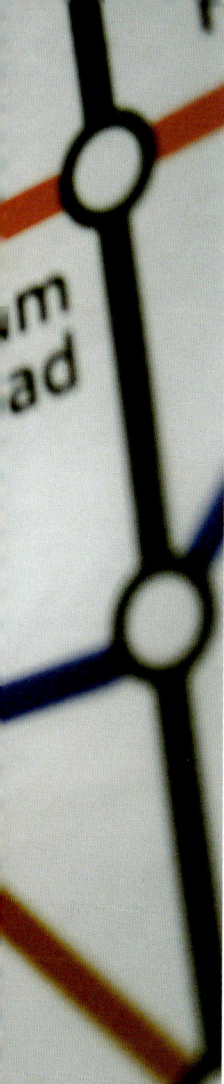

cityFacts

Babysitting	104
Climate	104
Disabled	104
Driving	104
Emergencies	105
Entry Formalities	106
Lost and Found	106
Money Matters	106
Post Offices	107
Public Holidays	107
Safety	107
Telephone	107
Time	108
Tipping	108
Toilets	108
Tourist Offices	108
Tours	109
Transport	110
Voltage	112
Weights and Measures	112

Babysitting

In London, most large hotels can help you with babysitting arrangements. Universal Aunts is an agency with over 80 years of experience (☎7738 8937, www.universalaunts.co.uk). Another reputable firm is Sitters (☎7915 3000, www.babysitters.co.uk).

Climate

Britain's weather is variable, changing quickly from grey and wet to sunny at any time of the year (or of the day). Play safe and take a waterproof or carry an umbrella.

Disabled

The disabled are well cared for in London. Artsline offers them a complimentary information and advice service on all aspects of the entertainment scene, ☎7388 2227, www.artsline.org.uk. For special accommodation, get in touch with Holiday Care Service, Hawkins Suite, Enham Palace, Enham Alamein, Andover, Hampshire, SP11 6JS, ☎0845 124 9971, www.holidaycare.org.

The Airbus between Heathrow and central London is equipped to handle wheelchairs, as is the Stationlink bus connecting all the mainline stations and the Docklands Light Railway; special Mobility Buses with wheelchair access run on various routes throughout London. Information on the above transport is available from Transport for London, ☎7027 5823/24, www.tfl.gov.uk. London Transport can provide an Underground map in Braille.

Driving

A congestion charge of £8 each weekday is imposed on motorists entering central London. For a map of the area (extended in February 2007) see www.london.com. To pay the charge, ☎ 0845 900 1234.

It's best to avoid driving in the centre, as parking spaces are practically impossible to find. Illegally parked cars may be clamped or towed away. Parking restrictions are shown by yellow lines painted on the roadsides, and spaces provided for borough residents are strictly controlled. A meter, if you can find one, is usually only for a maximum of two hours. London does have some public car parks, however, notably the 880-space facility at Park Lane on the Marble Arch traffic circle. (There is also a 24-hour petrol station at 83 Park Lane.)

You can download a free map of car parks from www.ncp.co.uk. For theatre parking, reduced-price vouchers are available when you book a ticket at any of the West End box offices.

Car hire. Renting a car in Britain is no problem. All you need is a passport and driver's licence. There may be minimum and maximum age requirements. If you pay with a credit card you avoid having to put down a big cash deposit.

Yield to pedestrians at "zebra crossings", marked by stripes on the roadway and flashing lights: they have right of way as soon as they step onto the crossing.

Unless otherwise indicated, speed limits are 30 mph (48 kph) in built-up areas, 60 mph (96 kph) on highways and 70 mph (113 kph) on motorways and dual carriageways.

Petrol (gasoline) is measured in both Imperial gallons and litres. You can usually pay by credit card.

Emergencies

If it's a matter of life or death, dial 999 (police, fire brigade or ambulance). You can dial free from any phone box and need neither coins nor a phonecard to reach the operator. Otherwise you can be treated at one of the 24-hour hospital casualty departments. Ask your hotel for the nearest or for the name of a doctor.

Free medical treatment is available from the National Health Service for citizens of the European Union (EU) and countries with reciprocal arrangements with Britain. Otherwise, you should see a private doctor for treatment and medical prescriptions. Before leaving home, check to see if your health insurance will cover you abroad. If not, it's wise to get coverage for your trip.

Walk-in service:
Medical Express 117A Harley Street, London W1, ☎7499 1991

Late-opening pharmacies:
Bliss Chemist 5 Marble Arch, ☎7723 6116, 9am–midnight

Boots the Chemist Piccadilly Circus, ☎7734 6126, Mon–Fri 8am–midnight, Sat, Sun 9am–midnight

Entry Formalities

Visitors from outside the EU need a passport. Citizens of the USA, Japan and most Commonwealth and South American countries do not require a visa.

Duty-free allowances on goods purchased outside the EU and brought into the UK are (for visitors over 17):
- 200 cigarettes or 50 cigars or 250 grams tobacco;
- 1 litre spirits over 22% or
- 2 litres dessert wine not exceeding 22% and sparkling wine, and
- 2 litres table wine;
- 60 cc perfume and 250 ml toilet water.

The allowance for goods bought in the EU corresponds essentially to whatever is reasonable for your personal consumption.

Lost and Found

For property lost on a bus or in the tube or a black taxi, call in at:
Transport for London Lost Property Office, 200 Baker Street, NW1, Mon–Fri 8.30am–4.30pm, ☎7918 2000.

If you do not recover the property and wish to make a claim to your insurance company, be sure that you declare the loss to the police.

Money Matters

Banks are open Monday to Friday 9.30am–3.30 or 4.30pm, and some open on Saturday morning. Foreign currency exchange offices generally keep longer hours.

Credit cards The major cards are accepted nearly everywhere in London, though the retailer may not appreciate your using it to pay for goods under £10. You can use credit cards such as American Express, Mastercard and Visa to get cash from ATM machines: you'll need to know your PIN code. A commission is charged.

Currency: One pound (£) = 100 pence (p). Notes range from £5 to £50, and coins from 1p to £2.

Travellers cheques: These—as well as foreign currency—are best changed in a bank to avoid the fees of a currency exchange, hotel or shop. Be sure to have some cheques in small denominations in case you run short of cash towards the end of your visit.

Post Offices

Normally open Monday to Friday 9am to 5.30pm and until 12.30pm on Saturday.

After hours, stamps are available from vending machines outside the post office, as well as from many shops.

Faxes can be sent from many post offices.

There are plenty of cybercafés in London, particularly around Trafalgar Square.

Public Holidays

If public holidays fall on a Sunday, the Monday is taken as a holiday. Many shops now stay open on official holidays.

January 1 *New Year's Day*
December 25 *Christmas Day*
December 26 *Boxing Day*

Movable: Good Friday, Easter Monday.
Bank holidays: first and last Mondays in May, and the last Monday in August.

Safety

As in all big cities, passports, travel tickets, travellers cheques and any other valuables should be deposited in your hotel safe until required. Carry the necessary cash for the day and a credit card, preferably not in your wallet or handbag.

Be forewarned of the dangers that traffic poses to the pedestrian. Britain drives on the left. The situation is especially complicated in one-way streets. Be sure to take heed of the notice printed in white at pedestrian crossings, warning either "Look left" or "Look right." Drivers generally stop as soon as they see a pedestrian waiting at a crossing.

Telephone

Phone numbers in inner London consist of 8 figures beginning with 7; in outer London they begin with 8. The long-distance area code for both areas is (020). The international access code is 00.

British Telecom (BT) and other private telephone companies have their own phone booths that accept coins, credit cards or selected telephone charge cards. BT phonecards are obtainable from post offices, newsagents and other shops.

Time
Britain operates on Greenwich Mean Time (GMT) from the last Sunday in October to the last Sunday in March, when the clocks are put forward an hour for summer time.

Tipping
Some restaurants automatically add 10–15% service charge to your bill while others leave it up to you to add a gratuity. Scrutinize the menu and the small print on the bill to see what the policy is—there's no point in tipping twice, although a little extra for especially good service will not go amiss. Tipping is not required in cafés or pubs, though customers often "buy a drink" for the person serving, which will be taken in cash.

Taxi drivers and hairdressers will expect a tip of at least 10 per cent, and porters, chambermaids and restroom attendants appreciate a small gratuity.

Toilets
Public "loos" are to be found in department stores, cafés, parks and squares, and in all public buildings. At train stations, you may have to insert a coin into a turnstile. Increasingly, coin-operated "Loomatic" toilets are being installed.

Tourist Information Offices
British & London Visitor Centre: 1 Lower Regent Street, Piccadilly Circus, SW1. Mon 9.30am–6.30pm, Tues–Fri 9am–6.30pm, Sat, Sun 10am–5pm (Oct–May 10am–4pm) ☎ 08701 566 366. Information on travel throughout Britain, as well as London theatre bookings.
Visit London: www.visitlondon.com
Information Centres: Victoria Station Forecourt; Heathrow Airport Terminals 1, 2, and 3 Underground Station Concourse; Terminal 3 Arrivals Concourse; Waterloo International Terminal Arrivals Hall; Liverpool Street Underground Station; Selfridges department store; St Paul's Churchyard EC4, ☎ 7332 1456.

Offices open daily (except Selfridges) 8 or 8.30am–7pm or later; shorter hours weekends.

Tours

Bus Tours. Double-decker sightseeing buses leave regularly from a number of central pick-up points, including Piccadilly Circus, Victoria, Marble Arch and Baker Street. Commentaries are given in several languages, either live or recorded.

You can also do your own tour on a regular city bus: Nos. 11, 15 and 38 go past the most landmarks.

London Transport buses offer a London by Night Bus Tour. Departures from Victoria Station at 7 or 9pm; from Piccadilly Circus at 7.35 or 9.35pm.

Boat Tours. Innumerable pleasure boats ply the Thames offering commentaries of the river scene, running downstream to Greenwich, the Docklands and the Thames Flood Barrier, and upstream, spring to autumn, to Kew and Hampton Court Palace. Lunch, dinner and disco cruises are also available. Inquire at Westminster, Tower Bridge or Charing Cross piers, or check the listings magazines for details. A one-day Discoverer ticket can be purchased at the piers, entitling you to discounts on entrance fees to six riverside attractions. For details, ☎7987 1185.

From April to September, you can also drift along historic Regent's Canal in a barge. Boarding points are Little Venice and Camden Lock. London Waterbus, ☎7482 2660, www.londonwaterbus.com.

Bicycle Tours. Three-hour tour of London led on weekends at 2pm by the London Bicycle Tour Company, Gabriel's Wharf. Reservations: ☎7928 6838.

Walking Tours. Discover the London of Dickens, Shakespeare, the Beatles or Jack the Ripper. Walks on many special themes are organized by Original London Walks (☎7624 3978), Secret London Walks (☎8881 2933, www.secretlondonwalks.co.uk) and Open House Architecture (☎7380 0412, www.londonopenhouse.org). The listings magazines give each day's programme.

Transport

www.tfl.gov.uk
Information Centres: Liverpool Street, Piccadilly Circus and Heathrow Terminal 123 tube stations; Euston, Victoria rail stations, Victoria coach station.
24-hour information line: 7222 1234; Recorded information: 7222 1200
Oyster pre-paid smart card: tfl.gov.uk/oyster or call 0845 330 9876

Underground. The Underground (or "Tube") is very efficient provided you avoid the weekday rush hours of 7.30 to 9.30am and 4.30 to 6.30pm. The tube functions from 5.30am to just after midnight.

Bus. Request the All London Bus Map for Greater London at one of the information centres listed under Tourist Information Offices, p. 108. Be sure to note details of late night buses (indicated by an "N" or an owl).

Remember that the British are extremely polite and board buses in an orderly fashion, so take your place in the queue.

Docklands Light Railway (DLR). This system of driverless trains connects with the tube system—underground at Bank and above ground at Tower Gateway (near Tower Hill station). If you're travelling on a single ticket, transfer from the Underground to the DLR at Bank to avoid having to leave the tube network and pay a second fare.

Special travel packages. The cheapest and most practical way to travel is with a pre-paid Oyster card, to be touched in at the start of your journey and touched out at the end. This guarantees you always pay the minimum fare (£1 single). Cards can be ordered online (tfl.gov.uk/oyster), at tube station ticket offices, travel information centres or tel. 0845 330 9876. Otherwise, tube tickets are available in a money-saving carnet of 10, but it will probably be more economical to buy one of the special Travelcards:

All-Zone Visitor Travelcard. This is a good solution if you plan to travel to the outlying corners of London every day (Heathrow, Richmond, Kew, etc.); it's only obtainable outside Britain through a local travel agent or agents for British Rail Intl. Available for 1, 3, 4 or 7 days, it covers all travel in all distance zones on the Underground, buses, DLR and British Rail Network South East. It comes with a booklet of discount coupons for London museums. No photo required.

Off-peak Travelcard. Valid after 9.30am for 1 or 7 days or a weekend for the above-mentioned means of transport. The 7-day card requires a photo. The Travelcard is on sale at all tube stations, London Transport Travel Information Centres, and selected London newsagents, and there is a choice of distance zones at different prices. It offers the flexibility of purchasing a card for the least expensive zones 1 and 2 if you don't plan to budge from central London. Family Travelcard also available.

LT Card. Essentially the same as the Off-peak Travelcard but with no time restrictions.

Taxis. Even if you're economizing, you may have need of a taxi from time to time, particularly after a late night on the town. Drivers of the Black Cabs (now appearing in other colours as well) know every corner of the city intimately. You'll be charged the standard fare shown on the meter for any trip inside London, with supplements for luggage or extra passengers. Pick up a taxi at one of the many ranks, phone for one on 7272 0272 or 7253 5000, or hail one in the street if its yellow sign is lit, indicating it's free.

Minicabs. Unlike the Black Cabs, minicabs are not licensed and may not legally solicit clients in the street. You will need to look under "minicabs" in the Yellow Pages telephone directory. Minicabs have no meters, so you should ascertain the fare before you ride, and it is well if you know the general route to be taken. Minicabs are generally cheaper than licensed taxis and indeed can be a good solution if you are, say, a group of four wishing to go to Hampton Court Palace. GLH Car Service, ☏8883 5000, has been in business for over 30 years. Female clients of Lady Cabs, ☏7272 33 00, can specify if they want a female driver.

From Heathrow. You can board the tube to central London right at the airport (Piccadilly line). The journey takes about 40 minutes. The fast Heathrow Express train, direct to Paddington Station, leaves every 15 minutes. Journey time from Terminals 1, 2 and 3: 15 min; 20 min from Terminal 4. You can purchase a ticket in advance from a machine in the baggage reclaim area. The Airbus leaves for Kings Cross Station at 20-minute intervals, with stops along the way. A taxi will cost at least £40.

From Gatwick. The fastest way to Victoria train station is by Gatwick Express, a non-stop train leaving every 15 minutes. The journey takes 30 minutes. British Rail's Thameslink runs to King's Cross, Blackfriars and London Bridge, leaving every half-hour during the day and every hour in the evening. Flightline 777 coach service to Victoria Coach Station takes an average of 70 minutes.

From London City Airport. Shuttle bus to Liverpool Street Station takes 25 minutes; shuttle bus to Canary Wharf, boarding point for the DLR.

From Stansted Airport. Train to Liverpool Street Station takes about 40 minutes; National Express bus to Victoria, 80 minutes.

From Luton Airport. Rail and coach link to King's Cross 45 to 60 minutes; coach to Victoria 75 to 90 minutes.

Long-distance coach. If you're thinking of spending a day outside the capital, check at the British & London Visitor Centre or one of the tourist information centres about the regularly scheduled intercity coaches. Alternatively, you can go to Victoria Coach Station (164 Buckingham Palace Road, SW1, open daily 6am to 11.30pm) or contact one of the main coach companies such as National Express (☎08705 808080, www.nationalexpress.com) or Green Line Coaches (☎0870 608 7261, www.greenline.co.uk). Tickets are sold on board, and prices are nearly always cheaper than the train.

The British & London Visitor Centre and tourist information centres can also advise you about guided coach tours to traditional attractions such as Stratford-upon-Avon, Kew Gardens, Hampton Court Palace, etc.

Inter City Rail. For trips out of London, the mainline stations serve Britain's cities and regions as follows:

Euston for Stratford-upon-Avon, the Midlands, Glasgow;
King's Cross for Cambridge, York and Edinburgh;
Liverpool Street for Cambridge, Colchester, Ipswich and Norwich;
Paddington for Oxford, Bath and the West Country;
Victoria for Gatwick, Brighton, Canterbury and Dover;
Waterloo for Eurostar to continent (until 13.11.2007), Winchester, Salisbury, Bournemouth and Portsmouth.
St Pancras for Eurostar from 14.11.2007. Information ☎08705 186 186
For inquiries on national rail lines, ☎08457 484 950.

Stationlink buses make the circuit of all the railway stations hourly, seven days a week. They connect with the Airbus running between Central London and Heathrow. Brochure and information available from London Transport's information centres (see p. 109).

Voltage

240 volts, 50 cycle AC. Plugs have three flat prongs, so American and European appliances require an adaptor. Most hotel rooms have a socket for 110-volt shavers.

Weights and Measures

Britain is slowly converting to the metric system. TV weather forecasters give degrees in Celsius and Fahrenhei. In pubs the beer is still pulled by the pint.

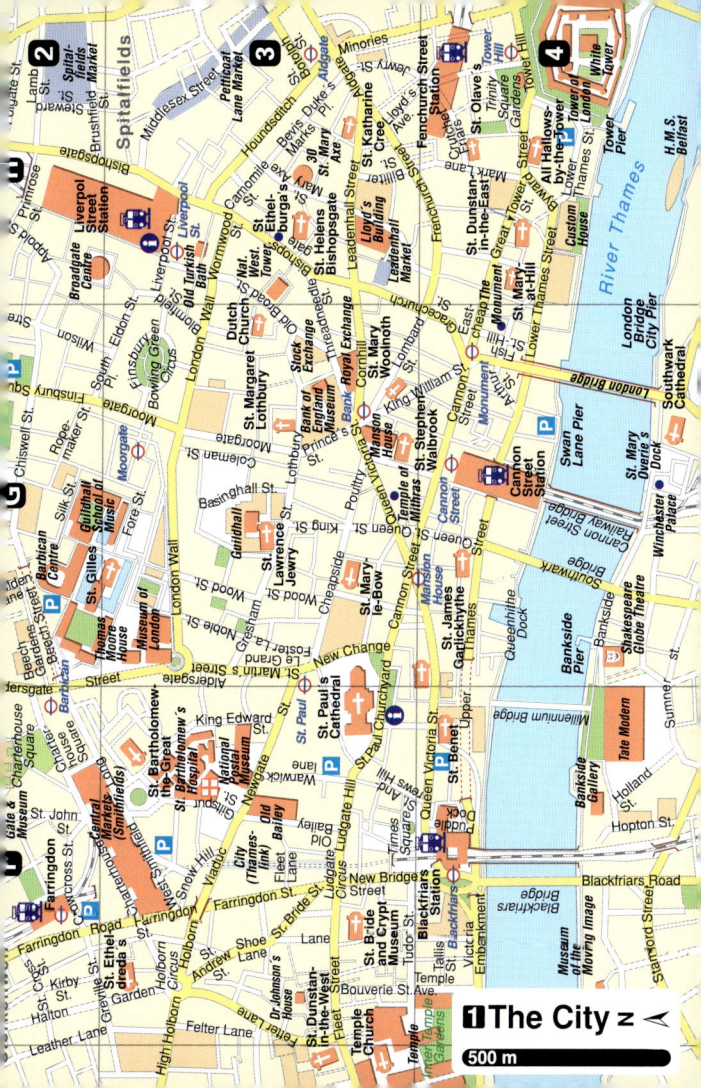

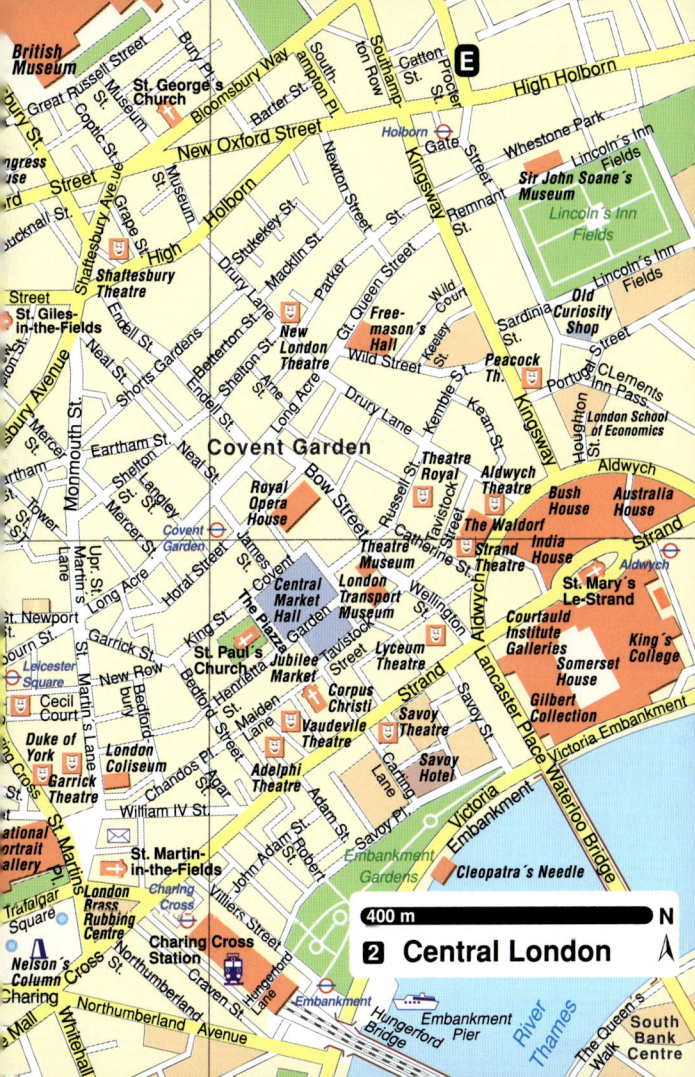

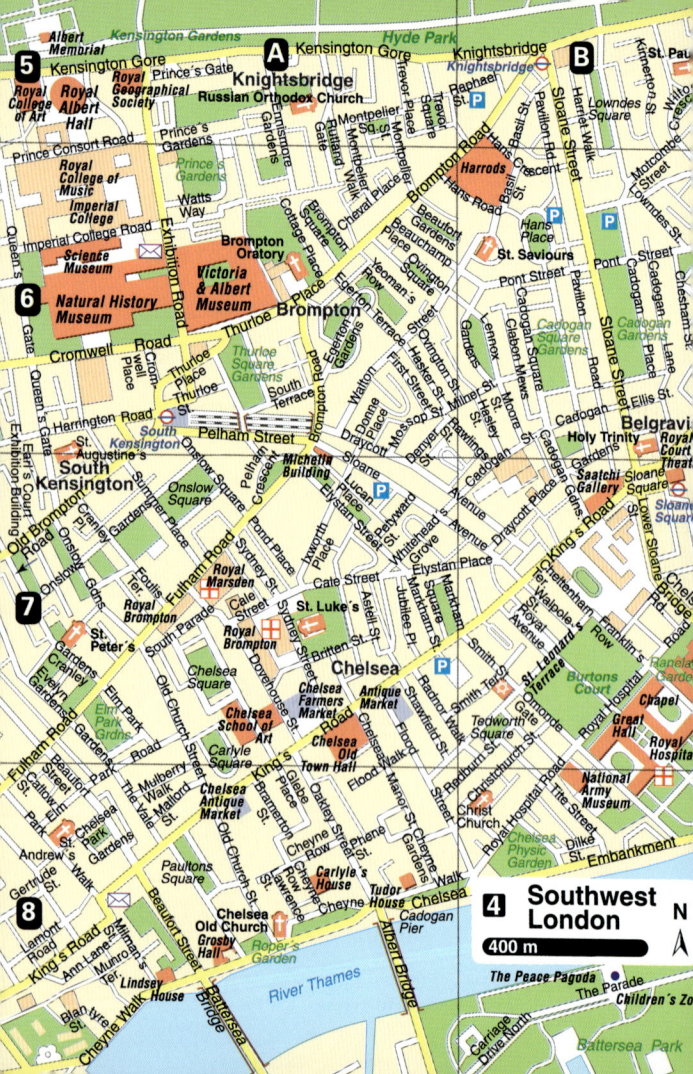

INDEX

Albert Memorial 54
Apsley House 46–47
BA London Eye 37, 62
Bank of England
  Museum 19
Bankside Power
  Station 61
Banqueting House 41
Barbican Arts
  Centre 96
Battersea Park 53
Bethnal Green Museum
  of Childhood 70
Bishopsgate 72
Bond Street 30
Bramah Tea & Coffee
  Museum 60–61
Brick Lane 57, 70, 72
British Museum 28
Brunel Engine House &
  Tunnel Exhibition
  58–59, 64
Buckingham Palace 46
Cabinet War Rooms 42
Cambridge 78–79
Camden Market 56
Canterbury 79
Carnaby Street 30
Charing Cross 41
Cheapside 22
Chelsea Physic
  Garden 53
Chelsea Royal
  Hospital 53
Chessington World of
  Adventures 37
Chiswick House
  76–77
Christ Church,
  Spitalfields 70
Clarence House 45

Clink Prison Museum
  37, 64
Clockmakers'
  Museum 20
Clubs 97
Courtauld Gallery 33
Covent Garden 32–33
Dali Universe 62
Dennis Severs' House 68
Department stores
  48–49
Design Museum 59
Dickens's House 27–28
Docklands 70–71
Dr Johnson's House 17
Estorick Collection 77
Fashion 49
Florence Nightingale
  Museum 63
Fortnum & Mason 32, 49
Geffrye Museum 69
Gilbert Collection 33
Globe Theatre 61–62, 64
Guildhall 19–20
Guildhall Art Gallery 20
Hampstead Heath
  77–78, 84
Hampton Court Palace
  79–80
Harrods 49, 51, 54
Hatfield House 80–81
Highgate 84
Historic Maritime
  Greenwich 71
HMS Belfast 59
Holland Park Open Air
  Theatre 98
Houses of Parliament 42
Hyde Park 37, 50
Imperial Institute
  Tower 54

Imperial War
  Museum 63
Inns of Court 26–27
Keats House 84
Kensington Gardens
  37, 50
Kensington Palace 50
Kenwood House 84, 98
Kew Gardens 78
King's Road 52
Knightsbridge 51
Leeds Castle 81
Leicester Square 32, 35
Liberty plc 30
London Aquarium
  37, 63
London Coliseum 96
London Dungeon
  37, 60
London Oratory 54
London Zoo 29, 36
London's Transport
  Museum 33
Madame Tussauds 28
Markets 56–57
Marks & Spencer 30, 49
Medieval city 24–25
Millennium Bridge 62
Mind the Gap 32
Monument, The
  20–21, 22
Museum of London 19
National Gallery 40
National Portrait
  Gallery 40
Natural History
  Museum 36, 52
Notting Hill 50–51
Old Bailey 18
Oxford 81–82
Oxford Street 29–30

INDEX

Petticoat Lane 57, 69–70
Piccadilly Circus 31
Portobello Road 56
Priory Church of
  St Bartholomew
  the Great 18
Pubs 74–75
Pudding Lane 22
Regent's Park 28
Regent's Park Open Air
  Theatre 98
Roman London 24
Royal Academy of
  Arts 96
Royal Albert Hall 54, 96
Royal Botanic
  Gardens 78
Royal Exchange 22
Royal Opera House 96
Saatchi Gallery 52–53
Sadler's Wells 96
Salisbury 82
Science Museum 36, 52
Selfridges 30, 49

Shakespeare's Globe
  Theatre and
  Exhibition 61–62, 64
Sherlock Holmes
  Museum 29
Shopping 48–49
South Bank Centre 96
Southwark Cathedral 60
Spencer House 45–46
Spitalfields 57, 72
St Bride's 16–17
St James's Church 31
St James's Palace 43–45
St James's Park 43
St Martin-in-the-Fields
  40
St Mary-le-Bow 22
St Paul's 18, 22
St Stephen Walbrook
  19, 22
Stonehenge 82
Stratford-upon-Avon 83
Tate Britain 43
Tate Modern 36–37, 62

10 Downing St 41–42
Thames Barrier 71
Thames Path 64
Theatre 96–98
Theatre Museum 33
Tower Bridge 21
Tower of London 21, 37
Trafalgar Square 39
Tudor London 25
V&A Museum 51
Wallace Collection 29
Wellington Arch 47–50
Wellington Museum 46
Westminster Abbey 42
Wetland Centre 78
Whitechapel Art
  Gallery 70
Whitechapel Road 72
Whitehall 40–41
Windsor Castle 83
Winston Churchill's
  Britain at War
  Experience 60
Woburn Abbey 83

General Editor: Barbara Ender
Layout: Luc Malherbe
Litho: Christine Bourgeois
Photo credits: Guy Minder except: hemis.fr/Wysocki pp. 6, 17, –/Gardel: pp. 13, 56 (r), –/Derwal p. 57 (r); CORBIS pp. 25, 74, 101; Barbara Ender p. 29; Christine Osborne Pictures pp. 47, 77; Leonie Mann p. 48; S. Cordaiy Photolibrary p. 63; Life File/Emma Lee p. 80; ©istockphoto.com/Christopher Steer p. 57(l), –/angelhell p. 100 (spool)
Maps: Elsner & Schichor, JPM Publications

Copyright © 2007 JPM Publications S.A., 12, avenue William-Fraisse, 1006 Lausanne, Switzerland
information@jpmguides.com — www.jpmguides.com

All rights reserved. No part of this book may be reproduced or transmitted in any form or by any means, electronic or mechanical, including photocopying, recording or by any information storage and retrieval system without permission in writing from the publisher.

Every care has been taken to verify the information in the guide, but neither the publisher nor his client can accept responsibility for any errors that may have occurred. If you spot an inaccuracy or a serious omission, please let us know.

Printed in Switzerland – 11562.00.1438, Weber/Bienne – **Edition 2007–2008**